# THE CHIEF JUSTICE OF THE

# UNITED STATES

# THE CHIEF JUSTICE OF THE UNITED STATES

## STEVEN RUTKUS
### AND
## LORRAINE H. TONG

**Novinka Books**
*New York*

Copyright © 2007 by Nova Science Publishers, Inc.
One College Avenue
Williamsport, PA 17701-5799

For permission to use material from this book please contact us:
Telephone 631-231-7269; Fax 631-231-8175
Web Site: http://www.novapublishers.com

### NOTICE TO THE READER

The Publisher has taken reasonable care in the preparation of this book, but makes no expressed or implied warranty of any kind and assumes no responsibility for any errors or omissions. No liability is assumed for incidental or consequential damages in connection with or arising out of information contained in this book. The Publisher shall not be liable for any special, consequential, or exemplary damages resulting, in whole or in part, from the readers' use of, or reliance upon, this material.

Independent verification should be sought for any data, advice or recommendations contained in this book. In addition, no responsibility is assumed by the publisher for any injury and/or damage to persons or property arising from any methods, products, instructions, ideas or otherwise contained in this publication.

This publication is designed to provide accurate and authoritative information with regard to the subject matter covered herein. It is sold with the clear understanding that the Publisher is not engaged in rendering legal or any other professional services. If legal or any other expert assistance is required, the services of a competent person should be sought. FROM A DECLARATION OF PARTICIPANTS JOINTLY ADOPTED BY A COMMITTEE OF THE AMERICAN BAR ASSOCIATION AND A COMMITTEE OF PUBLISHERS.

LIBRARY OF CONGRESS CATALOGING-IN-PUBLICATION DATA
Chief justice / Steven Rutkus, editor.
    p. cm.
Includes index.
ISBN 13 978-1-60021-225-3
ISBN 10 1-60021-225-5
1. United States. Supreme Court. 2. Judges--United States. I. Rutkus, Denis Steven.
KF8742.C48                                                                        2006
347.73'2634--dc22                                                         2006014392

*Published by Nova Science Publishers, Inc.* ✦ *New York*

# CONTENTS

# PREFACE<sup>*</sup>

The lifetime appointment of the Chief Justice of the United States is an event of major significance in American politics because of the enormous power that the Supreme Court exercises as the highest appellate court in the federal judiciary. The Chief Justice, like each of the Court's other eight Justices, casts one vote when the Court rules on cases. However, the Chief Justice is also "first among equals" and exercises a unique leadership role as the presiding officer of the Court, as the manager of the Court's overall operations, and as head of the federal judicial branch of government. There is no formal list of qualifications for the job; the Constitution's only mention of the Chief Justice is as presiding officer of the Senate during an impeachment trial of the President. Chief Justice appointments occur infrequently, with only 16 individuals having served in that position since 1789 —an average tenure of 13½ years per Chief Justice.

The process for appointing a Chief Justice is the same as for appointing Associate Justices and typically involves a sharing of responsibilities between the President, who nominates the Justices, and the Senate, which provides "advice and consent." (Exceptions to this have been rare instances when the President has made temporary "recess appointments" to the Court, which do not require the Senate's approval.) Vacancies on the Court can occur as a result of death, retirement, or resignation of a Justice. Chief Justice nominees may be selected from the ranks of sitting Associate Justices (as three of the 16 Chief Justices were) or from outside the Court, with each approach, from the perspective of the President, having certain advantages and disadvantages. The criteria that Presidents use in selecting a Supreme Court nominee vary, but typically involve policy and political considerations

---

<sup>*</sup> Excerpted from CRS Report RL32821 dated September 12, 2005.

as well as a desire to select a person with outstanding professional qualifications and unquestioned integrity. Leadership qualities may also be important when the Chief Justice position is involved. Presidents have also varied in the degree to which they have sought or used advice from Senators in selecting Supreme Court nominees.

As part of Senate consideration, the Judiciary Committee holds hearings on the nominee and votes on whether to report the nomination favorably, unfavorably, or without recommendation. Regardless of the outcome of that vote, the reporting of a Supreme Court nomination sends it to the full Senate for debate and a vote. Like the President, Senators may evaluate the nominee by such standards as professional excellence, integrity, and leadership qualities, but may also (again, as the President is free to do) focus on the nominee's judicial philosophy, views on constitutional issues, or how they believe the appointment might affect the Court's future direction on major legal and constitutional issues.

Under any circumstances, the appointment of a new Chief Justice will command the attention of Congress, especially the Senate, which votes on whether to confirm judicial nominations. Even more attention could be expected concerning such an event in the current political environment, in light of the controversy that has recently surrounded the judicial appointment process and the importance the President and Senators of both parties have attached to upcoming Supreme Court appointments.

# Chapter 1

# INTRODUCTION

The appointment of the Chief Justice of the United States is an infrequent event of major significance in American politics. The appointment of each Justice to the Supreme Court is significant because of the enormous judicial power that the Court exercises as the highest appellate court in the federal judiciary. The Chief Justice, like each of the Court's other eight Justices, casts one vote when the Court rules on cases. However, the Chief Justice also exercises a leadership role and wields unique influence, both within the Court itself and in the federal judiciary as a whole. Chief Justice appointments occur infrequently, with only 16 individuals having served in that position since 1789 — an average tenure of 13½ years per Chief Justice.[1]

On September 3, 2005, Chief Justice William H. Rehnquist died, after having served almost 19 years as Chief Justice.[2] He had been diagnosed with cancer in October 2004 and, although in ill health since then, had managed to lead the Court through its last term, which ended in late June 2005. His death came about two months after Associate Justice Sandra Day O'Connor had announced her intention to retire from the Court,[3] and only a few days before the scheduled start of confirmation hearings, on September 6, 2005, for her nominated successor, John G. Roberts, Jr., a U.S. appellate court judge. On September 6, President George W. Bush withdrew the Roberts nomination for the O'Connor seat and instead nominated Judge Roberts for Chief Justice.[4] At age 50, Judge Roberts, if confirmed by the Senate, would become the youngest Chief Justice at time of confirmation in more than 200 years.[5] Out of respect for the late Chief Justice, whose funeral was held on September 7, the Senate Judiciary committee postponed the start of its hearings on Judge Roberts's nomination to be Chief Justice until September 12.

Any Supreme Court nomination must be confirmed by the U.S. Senate, which, in recent Congresses, has been embroiled in controversies over various of the President's nominations to the lower federal courts. At times, Senate Democrats have accused President Bush of using his nominating power to appoint to the courts persons having controversial ideological agendas, and of making judicial appointments during Senate recesses in order to bypass the need for Senate confirmation.[6] Senate Republicans, in turn, have accused Senate Democrats of using their own ideological "litmus tests" to oppose certain judicial nominees and of making improper use of filibusters (extended debate as a delaying tactic) on the Senate floor to block Senate votes on circuit court nominees whom they oppose.[7]

Against this backdrop, a Supreme Court vacancy can be seen by Senators of both parties, at least to some extent, in an ideological context. Many highly controversial decisions of the Court in recent years have been closely decided, by 5-4 votes, appearing to underscore a longstanding philosophical or ideological divide in the Court between its more "liberal" and "conservative" members. Depending on their judicial philosophy, future appointees to the Court, Senators recognize, could have a potentially decisive impact on the Court's ideological balance and, as well, on whether past rulings of the Court will be upheld, modified, or overturned.[8]

All other things being equal, the appointment of a Chief Justice, owing to the responsibilities of the office and its symbolic importance, is foremost among the appointments that a President makes to the Supreme Court. Under any circumstances, it will command the attention of Congress, especially the Senate, which votes on whether to confirm judicial nominations. Even more attention is expected in the current political environment, in light of the controversy that has recently surrounded the judicial appointment process and the importance that the President and Senators of both parties have attached to upcoming Supreme Court appointments.

Other factors, moreover, can further complicate the appointment of a Chief Justice. The process, for instance, might become more contentious if the appointment of a new Chief Justice were seen as affecting the ideological balance of the Court, and thus galvanize opposition from Senators unhappy with the implications of the appointment. The process also might become more complicated if another Supreme Court appointment needs to be made at or around the same time as the Chief Justice appointment. This situation can arise, for instance, if a President nominates an Associate Justice to be Chief Justice, or if (as happened recently) an Associate Justice stepped down at about the same time as a Chief Justice vacancy were created — in either case, creating an Associate Justice vacancy for the President to fill.

This report is intended to help show what is unique about the office and to shed light on the process by which a Chief Justice is appointed. Hence, an initial section reviews the vast range of duties and responsibilities of the Chief Justice and the qualifications considered necessary for one to perform effectively in that office. A second section then examines the Supreme Court appointment process, focusing on the appointment of Chief Justices. At the end of this report, a table lists the names of all persons nominated for Chief Justice, from 1789 to the present, including their nomination dates and, if confirmed by the Senate, the dates of their confirmation, judicial oath, and end of service, as well as their ages at time of appointment and upon termination of service.

For a more detailed review of each stage in the Supreme Court appointment process, as it applies to Associate Justice as well as Chief Justice nominees, see CRS Report RL31989, *Supreme Court Appointment Process: Roles of the President, Judiciary Committee, and Senate.*

*Chapter 2*

# ROLES, RESPONSIBILITIES, AND QUALIFICATIONS OF THE CHIEF JUSTICE

## ROLES AND RESPONSIBILITIES

Only one of the Chief Justice's responsibilities is specified in the Constitution. Article I, Section 3, Clause 6 states that the Chief Justice shall serve as the presiding officer of the Senate during an impeachment trial of the President. Otherwise the Constitution does not mention the Chief Justice. The Judiciary Act of 1789, one of the first laws enacted by the first Congress, stipulated that the Supreme Court would consist of a Chief Justice and five Associate Justices.[9] In the two centuries that followed, Congress enacted legislation authorizing certain powers to the Chief Justice, and other duties have evolved over time through custom and practice.

The Chief Justice is the Court's most highly visible and identifiable figure —by virtue of the position's prominence and prestige, and the powers it has acquired by statute or through custom. The Chief Justice has been called the "first among equals" on the nine-member Court. Each Chief Justice brings an individual style of leadership that influences the way the Court operates, deliberates, and conducts its work. Moreover, the Chief Justice has considerable influence on the interactions that occur among the Justices. Many Chief Justices have left an indelible mark on the Court through their vision and leadership. Some, in retrospect, are admired for their constitutional scholarship, others are noted for their acumen in working effectively with the other Justices and the legislative and executive branches, and still others are recognized for administrative and organizational skills.[10]

The Chief Justice's most prominent role is that of presiding officer of the Court. In this capacity, the Chief Justice:

- presides at the private conference during which the Court decides which lower court decisions to accept from the large number received on appeal;
- presides over the public sessions, or hearings of cases, that come before the Court;
- chairs the private conference at which cases are discussed among the nine members of the Court and eventually decided by a vote of the Justices; and
- assigns, when in the majority, the writing of the Court's opinion on the case either to himself or to one of the Associate Justices.[11]

The Chief Justice is also manager of the Supreme Court's building and the overall operations of the Court. The administrative duties attendant to this role have increased over the years, commensurate with the growth of the nation, the sheer volume of cases presented to the Court, technological advances in court operations, and current security requirements.[12] Managerial tasks include approving the appointment of some court employees and the rules of the Supreme Court Library.

The Chief Justice, too, is the head of the federal judicial branch of government. In this capacity, key statutory duties of the Chief Justice include chairmanship of the Judicial Conference of the United States,[13] overall supervision of the Administrative Office of the United States Courts,[14] and chairmanship of the Board of the Federal Judicial Center.[15] Other duties include appointing two members of the Judiciary to the Commission on Executive, Legislative and Judicial Salaries, and reporting to Congress on changes in the Federal Rules of Criminal Procedure prescribed by the Supreme Court.[16]

As the head of the judicial branch, the Chief Justice is its spokesman and advocate. In this capacity, the late Chief Justice, William H. Rehnquist, took a leadership role in pressing for increases in judicial salaries and in funding for judicial branch operations. In his *2004 Year-End Report on the Federal Judiciary*, for instance, Chief Justice Rehnquist underscored his concern about the "funding crisis currently affecting the federal judiciary."[17] The tradition of the Chief Justice writing an annual report on the federal judiciary was begun by Chief Justice Warren E. Burger in 1970.[18]

The Chief Justice has statutory authority and responsibilities related to the circuit courts. By the order of the Supreme Court, the Chief Justice and the Associate Justices are allotted as circuit justices among the circuits. The Chief Justice is authorized to make such allotments when the Court is in recess.[19] Also by statute, the Chief Justice has authority to temporarily designate and assign " any circuit judge to act as a circuit judge in another circuit upon request by the chief judge or circuit justice of such circuit."[20] Further, he may assign any retired Chief Justice of the United States or Associate Justice of the Supreme Court to perform judicial duties in any circuit, including those of a circuit justice, as the designee agrees to undertake. The Chief Justice is to maintain a roster of retired justices who are willing and able to undertake special duties. [21]

Also by statute, the Chief Justice has several extra-judicial responsibilities. These include membership on the Board of Regents of the Smithsonian Institution,[22] the Board of Trustees of the National Gallery of Art,[23] and that of the Joseph H. Hirshhorn Museum and Sculpture Garden.[24] Further, the Chief Justice makes nonjudicial appointments, such as those to the National Commission on Reform of Federal Criminal Laws[25] and the National Historical Publications Commission.[26]

By tradition, the Chief Justice also performs a number of important ceremonial duties, such as administering the oath of office to the President.[27] In the international arena, the Chief Justice has engaged in judicial exchanges with foreign governments to promote understanding between judicial institutions and countries.[28]

Substitute leadership on the Court is provided for by federal statute whenever the Chief Justice "is unable to perform the duties of the office or the office is vacant." In such an event, the Chief Justice's "powers and duties shall devolve upon the associate justice next in precedence who is able to act, until such disability is removed or another Chief Justice is appointed and duly qualified."[29]

The late Chief Justice Rehnquist, in remarks made at Duke University on April 13, 2002, described his views of his office's responsibilities, and the potential impact that an individual can make while holding the office:

> A President brings to office his entire cabinet, from Secretary of State on down. But the Chief Justice brings to office no one but himself. He takes his seat with eight Associate Justices who are there already, and who are in no way indebted to him. By historic usage, he presides over the Court in open session, presides over the Court's conferences, and assigns the preparation of opinions in cases pending before the Court if he has voted with the majority. He also speaks on behalf of the federal judiciary in matters which pertain to it. But this structure obviously leaves great room for interplay among the members of the Court. Marshall and Taney were

dominant members of the Courts on which they served as Chief Justice; Chase and Vinson were not. Perhaps the best description of the office is to say that the Chief Justice has placed in his hands some of the tools which will enable him to be primus among the pares but his stature will depend on how he uses them.[30]

## QUALIFICATIONS FOR THE OFFICE

As noted, the office of Chief Justice requires that its occupant be able to perform in many demanding roles — as presiding officer of the Court, judge, constitutional scholar, statesman, consensus-builder, advocate, and administrator. Nevertheless, there is no formal list of qualifications for the job — not even a requirement that a nominee be a lawyer,[31] although every Justice to date has been a lawyer.

In recent decades, discussions in the Senate of the professional qualifications of judicial nominees in general often have focused on three aspects of a nominee's background — the nominee's integrity, professional competence, and judicial temperament. The breakdown of professional qualifications into these aspects has mirrored the three-pronged standard long used by the American Bar Association's (ABA's) Standing Committee on Federal Judiciary in evaluating federal judicial nominees on behalf of Presidents and the Senate Judiciary Committee.[32] In a booklet describing its evaluating role,[33] the ABA committee explains what its three standards measure. The criterion of professional competence, the committee writes, "encompasses such qualities as intellectual capacity, judgment, writing and analytical ability, knowledge of the law, and breadth of professional experience."[34]

As for nominees to the Supreme Court, the ABA committee comments that "the same factors considered with respect to the lower courts are relevant." In addition, however, the committee explains that its evaluation

> is based on the premise that the Supreme Court requires a person with exceptional professional qualifications. The significance, range and complexity of the issues considered by the Supreme Court, the importance of the underlying societal problems, the need to mediate between tradition and change and the Supreme Court's extraordinarily heavy docket are among the factors that require a person of exceptional ability."[35]

Besides the above-mentioned qualities that would be desirable in Supreme Court Justices in general, a number of additional intangible qualities as well would appear to be desirable, and even critical, to bring to the Chief Justice position. These would include leadership, scholarship, and consensus-building skills, as well as administrative abilities. Earlier experience on the Court may also be valuable, although, historically, such experience usually has not been critical in the selection of a Chief Justice nominee.[36]

John P. Frank, in *Marble Palace; the Supreme Court in American Life*, has articulated the view that a Chief Justice

> must get his real eminence not from the office but from the qualities he brings to it. He must possess the mysterious quality of leadership. In this respect the outstanding Chief was [John] Marshall, who for 35 years presided over a Court largely populated by Justices of an opposing political party. Moreover, his Court, because of the very newness of the Constitution it was expounding, dealt with some of the greatest questions of history.[37]

Former Chief Justice Charles Evans Hughes, in *The Supreme Court of the United States*, wrote:

> The Chief Justice as the head of the Court has an outstanding position, but in a small body of able men with equal authority in the making of decisions, it is evident that his actual influence will depend on the strength of his character and the demonstration of his ability in the intimate relations of the Judges.... Courage of conviction, sound learning, familiarity with precedents, exact knowledge due to painstaking study of the cases under consideration cannot fail to command that profound respect which is always yielded to intellectual power conscientiously applied.[38]

A decade prior to being appointed an Associate Justice in 1939, Felix Frankfurter defined the qualities that any member named to the Court should embody:

> The most relevant things about an appointee are his breadth of vision, his imagination, his capacity for disinterested judgment, his power to discover and suppress his prejudices.... Throughout its history, the Supreme Court has called for statesmanship — the gifts of mind and character fit to rule nations.[39]

These attributes would appear to be especially important for a Chief Justice, as the leader of the Court.

Apart from the personal qualities of individuals under consideration for appointment to be Chief Justice, external political factors may also play a part in determining whether these persons are a good "fit" for the appointment. Such factors would include the President's policy preferences, the Senate's party and ideological divisions, the composition of the current Court, and the candidates' chances for receiving Senate confirmation if nominated. The extent to which these factors can influence a President's selection of a nominee, as well as the Senate's decision on whether to confirm, are discussed in this report's next section.[40]

# Chapter 3

# PROCESS FOR APPOINTMENT OF A CHIEF JUSTICE

## BACKGROUND

## Brief Description of the Appointment Process

The modern-day process for appointing a Chief Justice is the same as that for appointing Associate Justices to the Court.[41] The need for a Supreme Court appointment arises when a vacancy occurs on the Court due to the death, retirement, or resignation of a Justice (or when a Justice announces the intention to retire or resign). At that point, it becomes the President's constitutional responsibility to select a successor to the vacating Justice. A Chief Justice appointment may be made only when there is, or is scheduled to be, a vacancy in the position of Chief Justice; the President may not use the occasion of an Associate Justice vacancy to appoint someone to replace a sitting Chief Justice.

Typically, candidates for the Supreme Court who are under serious consideration by the President will undergo a thorough investigation by the Administration into their private backgrounds, public record, and professional qualifications. In deciding whom to appoint, Presidents are free to receive advice from whomever they choose. The President may, but is not required to, seek advice from Members of the Senate. Advice may also come from many other sources, including House Members, officials in the President's administration, past and current Supreme Court Justices, party leaders, interest groups, and others.

The appointment process officially begins when the President selects someone to fill the Court vacancy. Except in rare cases of temporary recess appointments, the President will seek to give this person a lifetime appointment, which will require Senate consent. To obtain the Senate's approval, the President submits a written nomination of the person to the Senate. Usually on the same day it is received by the Senate, the nomination is referred to the Committee on the Judiciary. Immediately upon the President's announcement of a nominee, the Judicial Committee initiates its own intensive investigation into the nominee's background. When its investigation is completed, the Judiciary Committee holds hearings on the nomination, during which the nominee typically appears to testify and answer questions from Committee members. Then the committee votes on whether to report the nomination to the Senate and, if so, whether to report it favorably, unfavorably, or without recommendation. A report with a negative recommendation or no recommendation, like a favorable report, permits the nomination to go forward, to be considered by Senate as a whole, but it also alerts the Senate that a substantial number of committee members have reservations about the nominee.

In the next stage, consideration of the nomination by the full Senate is scheduled by the Senate majority leader, usually in consultation with the minority leader. If there is extended debate by opponents of the nomination, commonly called a filibuster, debate may be brought to a close by a "cloture" vote of three-fifths of the full Senate membership. (If three-fifths of the Senate's Members do not vote in favor of cloture, Senators opposing the nomination, even if in the minority, may use extended debate and opposition to cloture to prevent a vote on confirmation from taking place — a scenario, however, which has played out that way only once in the past.) After Senate debate on the nomination is concluded, the Senate votes to confirm or disapprove the nomination, with confirmation requiring a majority vote. If the Senate votes in the negative on whether to confirm, the nomination is defeated, and a resolution of disapproval is forwarded to the President.

If the Senate votes to confirm the nomination, the secretary of the Senate transmits the resolution of confirmation to the White House, where the President signs a document, called a commission, officially appointing the individual to the Court. The commission, after being engraved at the Department of Justice with a date of appointment, and signed by the Attorney General, is delivered to the appointee, along with the oath of office. After receiving the commission, the appointee is sworn into office, marking the completion of the appointment process.[42]

A President also may make a Supreme Court appointment without the Senate's consent, when the Senate is in recess. Such "recess appointments," however, are temporary, with their terms expiring at the end of the Senate's next session. Historically, recess appointments to the Supreme Court have been rare (the last three occurring in the 1950s) and sometimes have been controversial, in part because they bypassed the Senate and its confirmation role.

## Past Chief Justice Appointments

Starting with John Jay of New York, who took his judicial oath of office on October 19, 1789, to the present day, 16 individuals (all men) have served as Chief Justice of the United States. Fifteen of the 16 received lifetime appointments, after being nominated by the President and then confirmed by the Senate. One of the 15, prior to his nomination, had received a "recess appointment" from the President to serve for a limited term. A 16th individual served as Chief Justice only by temporary recess appointment, without subsequently being confirmed by the Senate for a lifetime appointment. Eleven of the 16 Chief Justices had never served on the Supreme Court before their appointments, while the other five had earlier served on the Court as Associate Justices.[43]

Four Chief Justice nominees failed to receive Senate confirmation. One of them was the recess appointee already mentioned, who, after first receiving appointment by the President during a Senate recess, was subsequently nominated when the Senate was in session, only to be rejected by a Senate roll call vote.[44] The three others, in the face of significant opposition in the Senate, saw their nominations withdrawn by the President.[45]

Two other nominees to be Chief Justice were confirmed by the Senate, but declined the appointments. One of them was John Jay, who, after having already served as Chief Justice and then as governor of New York, was nominated to be Chief Justice a second time.[46] The other was an Associate Justice who was content to remain in that position after receiving Senate confirmation to be Chief Justice.[47]

## Constitutional Language on Supreme Court Appointments

Under the Constitution, Justices on the Supreme Court receive lifetime appointments, holding office "during good Behaviour."[48] Such job security in the federal government is conferred solely on Supreme Court Justices and judges in lower federal courts established by Congress under Article III of the Constitution.[49] By constitutional design, lifetime appointments are intended to insure the independence of the Supreme Court (as well as the lower federal courts) from the President and Congress.[50] Once Justices are confirmed, a President has no power to remove them from office. A Justice may be removed by Congress, but only through the difficult and involved process of impeachment. Only one Supreme Court Justice has ever been impeached (in an episode that occurred in 1804), and he remained in office after being acquitted by the Senate.[51] Many Justices serve for 20 to 30 years and sometimes are still on the Court decades after the President who nominated them has left office.

The procedure for appointing a Justice to the Supreme Court is provided for in the Constitution of the United States in only a few words. The "Appointments Clause" in the Constitution (Article II, Section 2, Clause 2) states that the President "shall nominate, and by and with the Advice and Consent of the Senate, shall appoint ... Judges of the supreme Court."[52] While the process of appointing Justices has undergone some changes over two centuries, its most essential feature — the sharing of power between the President and the Senate — has remained unchanged: To receive lifetime appointment to the Court, one must first be formally selected ("nominated") by the President and then approved ("confirmed") by the Senate.

## The Creation of a Vacancy or Prospective Vacancy on the Court

The need for a Chief Justice appointment arises when the position becomes vacant, due to death, retirement, or resignation, or when the Chief Justice announces the intention to retire or resign. It then becomes the President's constitutional responsibility to select a successor.[53] Historically, Justices have announced their retirements or resignations in letters to the President. In letters of this sort, outgoing Chief Justices have timed their departures in various ways — effective immediately, upon a specified future date, upon the qualification of a successor, or at the pleasure of the President.[54]

As noted above, a Supreme Court vacancy also could occur if a Justice were removed by Congress through the impeachment process, but no Justice has ever been removed from the Court in this way. A vacancy could occur, as well, upon the expiration of the term of a Justice who received a recess appointment from the President. However, the only recess-appointed Supreme Court Justice who was not later confirmed by the Senate, Chief Justice John Rutledge in 1795, resigned before his term expired.[55]

A vacancy on the Court is not necessarily created if a Justice becomes permanently disabled from performing the duties of the office. The vacancy, in that instance, is created only when the Justice either steps down on his or her own volition or dies in office. When a permanently disabled Justice declines to retire, no law or Court rule provides for his or her removal. While statutory procedures exist for lower courts to certify the permanent disability of a colleague,[56] none exists for the

Supreme Court.[57] Instead, the Court "relies on justices to determine when they are no longer fit to serve."[58] The President is empowered to appoint someone to take the place of a disabled Justice only when he or she, by death or retirement, vacates the position.

# PRESIDENT'S SELECTION OF A NOMINEE

## Criteria for Selecting a Nominee

The precise criteria used in selecting a Supreme Court nominee will vary from President to President. Two general motivations, however, appear to underlie the choices of almost every President, whether the appointment is for Chief Justice or for an Associate Justice seat. One motivation is to have the nomination serve the President's political interests (in the partisan and electoral senses of the word "political," as well as in the public policy sense); the second is to demonstrate that a search was successfully made for a nominee having the highest professional qualifications.

Virtually every President is presumed to take into account a wide range of political considerations when faced with the responsibility of filling a Supreme Court vacancy. For instance, most Presidents, it is assumed, will be inclined to select a nominee whose political or ideological views appear compatible with their own. "Presidents are, for the most part, results-oriented. This means that they want justices on the Court who will vote to decide cases consistent with the president's policy preferences."[59] The President also may consider whether a prospective nomination will be pleasing to the constituencies upon whom he especially relies for political support. For political or other reasons, such nominee attributes as party affiliation, geographic origin, ethnicity, religion, and gender may also be of particular importance to the President.[60] A President also might take into account whether the existing "balance" among the Court's members (in a political party, ideological, demographic, or other sense) should be altered. Another consideration will be the prospects for a potential nominee receiving Senate confirmation. Even if a controversial nominee is believed to be confirmable, an assessment must be made as to whether the benefits of confirmation will be worth the costs of the political battle to be waged.[61]

Most Presidents also want their Supreme Court nominees to have unquestionably outstanding legal qualifications. Presidents look for a high degree of merit in their nominees not only in recognition of the demanding nature of the work that awaits someone appointed to the Court, but also because of the public's expectations that a Supreme Court nominee be highly qualified.[62] With such expectations of excellence, Presidents often present their nominees as the best person, or among the best persons, available.[63]

Closely related to the expectation that a Supreme Court nominee have excellent professional qualifications are the ideals of integrity and impartiality in a nominee. Most Presidents presumably will be aware of the historical expectation, dating back to Alexander Hamilton's pronouncements in the *Federalist Papers*, that a Justice be a person of unquestioned integrity who is able to approach cases and controversies impartially, without personal prejudice.[64]

A President, however, may have additional concerns when the Supreme Court vacancy to be filled is that of the Chief Justice. Besides requiring that a candidate be politically acceptable, have excellent legal qualifications, and enjoy a reputation for integrity, a President might be concerned that his nominee have proven leadership qualities necessary to effectively perform the tasks specific to the position of Chief Justice. Such qualities, in the President's view, could include administrative and human relations skills, with the latter especially important in fostering collegiality among the Court's members. The President also might look for distinction or eminence in a Chief Justice nominee sufficient to command the respect of the Court's other Justices, as well as further public respect for the Court. A President, too, might be concerned with the age of the Chief Justice nominee, requiring, for instance, that the nominee be at least of a certain age (to insure an adequate degree of maturity and experience relative to the other Justices) but not above a certain age (to allow for the likely ability to serve as a leader on the Court for a substantial number of years).

The situation faced by President Dwight D. Eisenhower in 1953 is illustrative of the wide range of criteria a President might apply when deciding whom to appoint to fill a Chief Justice vacancy. On September 8, 1953, Chief Justice Fred M. Vinson died unexpectedly. Within days, the President, according to one news analysis, was being "urged by prominent members of his party to apply all sorts of different tests — political, geographical, personal, philosophical" — in deciding on a successor to Vinson. A major geographical consideration, which was said to favor the appointment of Earl Warren, governor of California, was that among the Court's eight remaining members there were "no representatives from the West, and of the fifty-six appointments to the Court since the beginning of the Civil War, only two [had] been from California."[65]

However, another factor, age, was said to favor former New York governor Thomas E. Dewey, who, at 51, was 11 years younger than Governor Warren. The reasoning urged upon the President by Dewey supporters was that "all other things being equal, the authority of a Chief Justice tends to increase with the duration of his service on the court." Hence, a younger-appointed Chief Justice might have more time "for his personality and character to leave a strong imprint on [the] Court's decisions" and to "develop strong lines of allegiance among the other justices."[66]

The news analysis noted that both Governors Dewey and Warren

> have distinguished legal and administrative records; both have impressive traits of character; both have strong personal and political claims on the President, but, in the last analysis, the question is: What test will President Eisenhower apply when he puts his mind to this momentous decision?[67]

Ultimately, the President appointed Governor Warren. President Eisenhower and his closest political advisers were agreed "that Warren's experience, leadership qualities, and administrative expertise constituted precisely the kind of medicine that the badly faction-rent Vinson Court needed." Moreover, they were "convinced that here was ... a bona fide 'middle-of-the-road' or 'moderate' Republican."[68]

In his memoirs, President Eisenhower noted that, from the beginning of his administration in 1953, he wanted the federal judges he selected to "command the respect, confidence, and pride of the population."[69] To that end, he set the following qualification standards for each judicial appointee:

- " ... character and ability would be the first qualifications to seek";
- Approval of the American Bar Association's Committee on Federal Judiciary and "the respect of the community in which he lived";
- A "thorough investigation of the prospective appointee's reputation and of every pertinent detail of his life" by the Federal Bureau of Investigation ;
- An upper age limit for initial appointment of 62 ("allowing a margin of a year or so if other qualifications were unusually impressive"); ! "General health";
- "Solid common sense," which would "exclude ... candidates known to hold extreme legal or philosophic views."[70]

As to Supreme Court appointments, Eisenhower recounted, another consideration was the past party affiliations of the Court's members. In 1953, before the death of Chief Justice Vinson, "eight of the nine members of the Court had been classed as Democrats before joining the Court and only one — Associate Justice Harold Burton — as a Republican. Naturally for the good of the country, I hoped eventually to achieve a better balance in this regard." However, he added, "I had no intention of selecting a chief justice merely on such a basis. My goal was a United States Supreme Court worthy of the high esteem of the American people."[71]

For the office of Chief Justice, Eisenhower recalled, additional factors had to be considered:

> A chief justice, I felt, should in addition to meeting all the criteria I had established for the selection of other judges, be a man of national stature, who had such recognized administrative ability as to promise an efficient conduct of the affairs of the Court and who could be expected to provide a leadership that would be favorably received by all of the courts of the land.[72]

Of various candidates for Chief Justice that immediately came to mind, the former President recalled, most were automatically eliminated either because of advanced age or a record of unsound health. These considerations, he noted, ruled out a number of members of the Court for elevation to Chief Justice, while two other Justices "represented what I thought were extreme views in matters that could be expected to come before the Court for decision."[73]

Early in his Administration, but after the appointment of Earl Warren as Chief Justice, President Eisenhower added another criterion to be applied specifically to the selection of Supreme Court Justices:

I told the Attorney General that I would not thereafter appoint anyone who had not served on a lower federal court or on a state supreme court. My thought was that this criterion would insure that there would then be available to us a record of the decisions for which the prospective appointee had been responsible. These would provide an inkling of his philosophy.[74]

In the remainder of his Administration, President Eisenhower made four additional Supreme Court appointments. Unlike Governor Warren, who had no prior judicial experience, Eisenhower's four subsequent appointees to the Court all had prior judicial service (three in the federal judiciary and one on a state supreme court).[75]

## The Role of Senate Advice

Historically, Presidents have varied in the degree to which they have sought or used advice from Senators in selecting Supreme Court nominees. It is a common, though not universal, practice for Presidents, as a matter of courtesy, to consult with Senate party leaders as well as with members of the Senate Judiciary Committee before choosing a nominee.[76] Senators who candidly inform a President of their objections to a prospective nominee may help in identifying shortcomings in that candidate or the possibility of a confirmation battle in the Senate, which the President might want to avoid. Conversely, input from the Senate might draw new Supreme Court candidates to the President's attention, or provide additional reasons to nominate a person who already is on the President's list of prospective nominees.[77]

As a rule, Presidents are also careful to consult with a candidate's home-state Senators, especially if they are of the same political party as the President. The need for such care is due to the longstanding custom of "senatorial courtesy," whereby Senators, in the interests of collegiality, are inclined, though not bound, to support a Senate colleague who opposes a presidential nominee from that Member's state. While usually invoked by home-state Senators to block lower federal court nominees whom they find unacceptable, the custom of "senatorial courtesy" has sometimes also played a part in the defeat of Supreme Court nominations.[78]

Sometimes, however, a President may deliberately limit the role performed by Senate advice in the selection of a Supreme Court nominee. In 1969, for instance, President Richard M. Nixon noted that in his selection of Warren E. Burger to be

Chief Justice, he had not received approval from the Senators of the state from which Burger had originally come (Minnesota) or the state in which he then resided (Virginia). "There were no political clearances in this case," the President declared, and there will be none for any judges to the Supreme Court that I appoint."[79] Further, the President stated that he told "all the Members of the Senate and the House, Democrat and Republican," to submit their recommendations for a Chief Justice nominee not to him directly, but through Attorney General John Mitchell. (In turn, the Attorney General would submit to the President "the case for each man," with the President then making the decision.) President Nixon explained that he "did not want to become personally involved in the contest, the very lively contest among several very well-qualified people for this position."[80]

Constitutional scholars have differed as to how much importance the framers of the Constitution attached to the word "advice" in the phrase "advice and consent." The framers, some have maintained, contemplated the Senate performing an advisory, or recommending, role to the President prior to his selection of a nominee, in addition to a confirming role afterwards.[81] Others, by contrast, have insisted that the Senate's "advice and consent" role was meant to be strictly that of determining, after the President's selection had been made, whether to approve the President's choice.[82]

Bridging the opposing schools of thought just noted, another scholar has asserted that the "more sensible reading of the term 'advice' is that it means that the Senate is constitutionally entitled to give advice to a president on whom as well as what kinds of persons he should nominate to certain posts, but this advice is not binding."[83] More recently, a similar view was expressed by the chairman of the Senate Judiciary Committee, Arlen Specter (R-PA), regarding the role of Senate advice on Supreme Court appointments. At a February 24, 2005, news conference, Senator Specter, in response to a question, stated that for a President,

> taking advice is not too hard as long as you get to make the final decision. And the Constitution doesn't say the President should do more than take advice. But the Constitution does say that there should be advice from the Senate.[84]

## Selecting from Within or Outside the Court

The President may select a Chief Justice nominee from within — i.e., from among the Court's Associate Justices — or from outside the Court.

Each option may present the President with different considerations, attractions and drawbacks.

## Choosing a Sitting Associate Justice to be Chief Justice

If the President's choice to be Chief Justice is a sitting Associate Justice, the latter must be nominated and confirmed again to the Court — this time to the position of Chief Justice. The appointment of an Associate Justice to be Chief Justice is often referred to as an "elevation."[85] The President is free to select any one of the Associate Justices to be Chief Justice, without regard to seniority. In the past, Presidents have sought to elevate a sitting Associate Justice to be Chief Justice on five occasions, and were successful on three of those occasions.[86]

Appointment of an Associate Justice to be Chief Justice, if successful, creates a vacancy in the Associate Justice position. Selecting a Chief Justice nominee from within the Court thus affords the President the opportunity, in conjunction with the Chief Justice appointment, to make a second Supreme Court appointment, to fill the vacancy created by the Associate Justice's elevation.

It has been suggested that selecting a Chief Justice from within the Court, and therefore being able to make two Court appointments, might appeal to a President if he is concerned with making the Court more in accord with his own values or vision for the Court.[87] Instead of selecting a Chief Justice nominee from outside the Court, and having only one appointment opportunity, a President, taking the Associate Justice option, could potentially, through carefully screening of nominee candidates, name two persons to the Court with views and values similar to his own. Moreover, the Associate Justice vacancy could be regarded as an opportunity to nominate a relatively young person to the Court, whose influence might be felt on the Court for years — and who himself or herself could, at some later point, be considered by a President for appointment to Chief Justice.

The two-appointment option, however, might pose political pose risks for a President, depending on the circumstances. Two nominations, for instance, might lead to two confirmation battles in the Senate, generating more conflict or controversy in Congress's upper chamber than the President would care to contend with. One Supreme Court appointment, even of a relatively controversial nominee, might not provoke widespread opposition in the Senate, if the appointment were not, by itself, seen to portend a significant change in the ideological "balance" of the Court's membership. By contrast, two Court appointments, made at the same time, might, if balance on the Court were seen to be at stake, galvanize the President's political opponents in the Senate to oppose either or both nominees.

When nominating someone from within the Court to be Chief Justice, the President does not have to wait for the Chief Justice nomination to be confirmed before nominating a successor to the Associate Justice being elevated. The Associate Justice nomination is made with the understanding that, before its new appointee can take office, the Associate Justice position must become vacant. This vacancy occurs only when the Chief Justice nominee steps down as Associate Justice, which he or she presumably will do only after receiving Senate confirmation to be Chief Justice.[88]

### Choosing Someone Outside the Court to be Chief Justice

If the President chooses someone from outside of the Court to be Chief Justice, there will be only one vacancy to fill and, therefore, only one nomination to make. Thirteen of the Court's past Chief Justices (including in this count the first Chief Justice, John Jay) were selected as nominees from outside the Court, although two of them had been Associate Justices prior to the time that they were nominated to be Chief Justice.[89]

A single Chief Justice nomination from outside the Court might seem the more desirable option to a President if he sees no clear potential leader or unifier among the Court's current Associate Justices. A President particularly might be reluctant to choose a Chief Justice nominee from among Associate Justices who are highly polarized or antagonistic to each other, as such an appointment might only worsen divisiveness within the Court.[90]

In 1969, when explaining his choice of Warren E. Burger, a circuit court of appeals judge, to be Chief Justice, President Richard M. Nixon noted that the option of selecting a nominee from within the Court had been considered by him on at least one occasion. The idea was raised, President Nixon said, by Associate Justice Potter Stewart, who, a few weeks earlier, had visited him at the White House. During their meeting, Justice Stewart said that "he felt that it would not be in the best interest of the Court to appoint a sitting judge on the Court to Chief Justice." The Justice explained, according to the President, that,

> generally speaking, because of the special role that the Chief Justice has to play as the leader of the Court, it would be very difficult to take a man from the Court and put him above the others. He said it would be better to bring a man from the outside rather than one from the Court. And with that he took himself out and asked me not to consider him.[91]

A Chief Justice nomination from outside the Court also allows the White House to concentrate its efforts to secure confirmation on one nomination, rather than on two. For the current President, George W. Bush, one analyst has suggested that a single nomination strategy for Chief Justice

> would make a tug of war between Mr. Bush and Senate Democrats more stark and more easily understood by the public. A single clash also could reduce the amount of bad blood generated and time consumed in the Senate, the chamber that is expected to take the lead on the President's Social Security proposal.[92]

## Recess Appointments to the Court

On 12 occasions in our nation's history (most of them in the nineteenth century), Presidents have made temporary appointments to the Supreme Court without submitting nominations to the Senate.[93] These occurred when Presidents exercised their power under the Constitution to make "recess appointments" when the Senate was not in session.[94] Historically, when recesses between sessions of the Senate were much longer than they are today, "recess appointments" served the purpose of averting long vacancies on the Court when the Senate was unavailable to confirm a President's appointees. However, the terms of these "recess appointments" were limited, expiring at the end of the next session of Congress (unlike the lifetime appointments Court appointees receive when nominated and then confirmed by the Senate). Despite the temporary nature of these appointments, every person appointed to the Court during a recess of the Senate, except one, ultimately received a lifetime appointment after being nominated by the President and confirmed by the Senate.[95]

The one Supreme Court Justice not to receive Senate confirmation after his recess appointment was a Chief Justice appointee — John Rutledge of South Carolina. Rutledge was one of President George Washington's first appointments to the Court as an Associate Justice in 1789. In February 1791, he resigned from that position, to become chief justice of South Carolina's supreme court. Rutledge then returned to the national scene when President Washington recess appointed him Chief Justice on July 1, 1795 (two days after nation's first Chief Justice, John Jay, stepped down upon being elected governor of New York). The appointment of Rutledge was made a few days after the 4th Congress began an adjournment that lasted more than five months.[96] On December 10, 1795, shortly after the Congress reconvened, President Washington nominated Rutledge for a lifetime appointment as Chief Justice.

Rutledge, however, was a controversial nominee, in large part because of a statement he had made on July 16, 1795 (after his recess appointment, but before receiving his commission) that was highly critical of the Jay Treaty with Great Britain, which the Senate had ratified three weeks earlier.[97] On December 15, less than a week after receiving the nomination, the Senate rejected Rutledge as Chief Justice by a roll call vote of 10 in favor of confirmation and 14 opposed.[98] In a December 28, 1795 letter to President Washington, from Charleston, South Carolina, Rutledge resigned his commission as Chief Justice, citing considerations of fatigue and ill health.[99] A documentary history of the early years of the Court said it was not clear if John Rutledge "knew that his nomination had been rejected when he wrote this letter."[100] Had Rutledge chosen not to resign, his recess appointment, under the Constitution, would have allowed him to serve to the end of the 1st session of the 4th Congress — June 1, 1796.[101]

Besides Rutledge in 1795, only one other Chief Justice received a recess appointment to that position — Earl Warren in 1953. The position had become vacant on September 8, 1953, upon the death of Chief Justice Fred M. Vinson. At the time of Vinson's death, Congress was in recess (having adjourned on August 3, and was not scheduled to reconvene until the start of its next session, in early January 1954. The Court also was in recess, but scheduled to start its next term shortly, on October 5, with highly controversial racial segregation cases scheduled to be argued before it. Reporting the death of Chief Justice Vinson, the *New York Times* noted that President Dwight D. Eisenhower could "either fill the vacancy by recess appointment or summon the Senate into special session to receive his appointment."[102]

On October 2, 1953, President Eisenhower recess appointed Earl Warren, the governor of California, to be Chief Justice, and three days later, on the first day of the Court's October 1953 term, the new Chief Justice was sworn into office. On January 11, 1954, shortly after the 83rd Congress convened for its second session, the President formally nominated Warren to be Chief Justice. Following two days of Senate Judiciary Committee hearings on the Chief Justice nomination and a favorable committee report, the nomination was confirmed by the Senate on March 1, 1954 by voice vote.

# CONSIDERATION BY THE SENATE JUDICIARY COMMITTEE

Although not mentioned in the Constitution, the Senate Judiciary Committee, for the last century and a half, has regularly played an important role midway in the process — after the President selects, but before the Senate as a whole considers the nominee. Since the end of the Civil War, almost every Supreme Court nomination received by the Senate has first been referred to and considered by the Judiciary Committee before being acted on by the Senate as a whole.[103]

Since the late 1960s, the Judiciary Committee's consideration of a Supreme Court nominee almost always has consisted of three distinct stages — a pre-hearings investigative stage, followed by public hearings, and concluding with a committee decision on what recommendation to make to the full Senate. For a detailed discussion of the Committee's pre-hearing stage, see CRS Report RL31989, *Supreme Court Appointment Process,* pp. 20-22.

## Hearings Stage

During the nineteenth century, the Judiciary Committee routinely considered Supreme Court nominations behind closed doors, with its deliberations during the twentieth century gradually becoming more public in nature. According to one expert source, the earliest Supreme Court confirmation hearings held in open session were those in 1916 for the nomination of Louis D. Brandeis to be an Associate Justice.[104] In 1925, Harlan F. Stone became the first Supreme Court nominee to appear in person and testify at his confirmation hearings. Neither the Brandeis nor the Stone hearings, however, served as binding precedents. Through the 1940s, the Judiciary Committee often declined to hold open confirmation hearings or to invite Supreme Court nominees to testify.[105]

In 1954, two days of hearing were held on the nomination of Earl Warren to be Chief Justice.[106] The hearings were scheduled in part to allow several relatively unknown persons from California an opportunity to state for the record why they opposed the California governor's appointment to the Court.[107] The nominee, however, did not appear to testify on his own behalf and was not invited by the committee to do so.

Hearings in 1955 on the Supreme Court nomination of John M. Harlan marked the beginning of a practice, continuing to the present, of each Court nominee testifying before the Judiciary Committee.[108] In keeping with this practice, the next person nominated to be Chief Justice, Associate Justice Abe Fortas in 1968, appeared at his confirmation hearings, to testify and respond to Senators' questions. The appearance of Justice Fortas before the committee on July 16, 1968 "marked the first time that a nominee to the Chief Justiceship ever had been heard by the Committee and the first time, except for Justices serving on a recess appointment, that a sitting Justice ever had been heard."[109] Likewise, the next two Chief Justice nominees, Warren Burger in 1969 and William H. Rehnquist in 1986, also appeared before the committee. The Rehnquist hearings were the first hearings on a Chief Justice nominee to be opened to gavel-to-gavel television coverage.[110]

## Reporting the Nomination

In modern practice, after holding hearings on a Supreme Court nomination, the Judiciary Committee meets in open session to determine what recommendation to "report" to the full Senate. The committee may report the nomination favorably, negatively, or make no recommendation at all.

Technically, the committee, if a majority of its members oppose confirmation, may decide not to report the nomination, to prevent the full Senate from considering the nominee. However, dating back at least to the 1880s, the Judiciary Committee's traditional practice has been to report even those Supreme Court nominations that were opposed by a committee majority, thus allowing the full Senate to make the final decision on whether the nominee should be confirmed.[111] A report with a negative recommendation or no recommendation permits the nomination to go forward, while alerting the Senate that a substantial number of committee members have reservations about the nominee.[112] The traditional practice of the Judiciary Committee to allow the full Senate to make the final decision, applies only to Supreme Court nominations, and not to judicial nominations in general. Historically, as well as in modern practice, lower court nominations (such as to U.S. district courts or U.S. circuit courts of appeals) are sometimes not reported by the Judiciary Committee, particularly if a nominee's confirmation is opposed by a Senator from the nominee's state.[113]

Reporting a Supreme Court nomination, in recent decades, almost always has included the transmittal of a written committee report, which presents the views both of committee members supporting and those opposing the nominee's confirmation. In such a fashion, the most recent Chief Justice nomination, of William H. Rehnquist in 1986, was reported favorably by the Judiciary Committee by a vote of 13-5, in a printed report, which included statements explaining the votes of the majority in favor and of the minority opposed to confirmation.[114]

By contrast, the previous Chief Justice nomination, of Warren E. Burger in 1969, was reported favorably by the committee, without a written report. During Senate consideration of the nomination, the absence of a written report from the Judiciary Committee prompted three Senators to express concerns. They maintained it was important for the Senate, when considering an appointment of this magnitude, to be able to consult a written report from the Judiciary Committee that provided a breakdown of any recorded votes by the committee and an explanation of the committee's recommendation regarding the nominee.[115]

## SENATE DEBATE AND CONFIRMATION VOTE

After the Judiciary Committee has reported a nomination, it is assigned an executive calendar number by the executive clerk of the Senate.[116] Consideration of the nomination is then scheduled by the Senate majority leader, usually in consultation with the minority leader.

## Criteria Used to Evaluate Nominees

Once the Senate begins debate on a Supreme Court nomination, many Senators typically will take the floor. Some, in their opening remarks, will underscore the importance of the Senate's "advice and consent" role, and the consequent responsibility to carefully determine the qualifications of a nominee before voting to confirm. Invariably, each Senator who takes the floor will state for the record his or her reasons for voting in favor of or against the nominee's confirmation.

The criteria used to evaluate a Supreme Court nominee are a personal, very individual matter for each Senator.[117] In their floor remarks, some Senators may cite a nominee's professional qualifications or character as the key criterion, others may stress the importance of the nominee's judicial philosophy or views on constitutional issues, while still others may indicate that they are influenced in varying degrees by all of these criteria. In recent decades, Senate debate on virtually every Supreme Court nomination has focused to some extent on the nominee's judicial philosophy, ideology, constitutional values, or known positions on specific legal controversies.

When evaluating a Chief Justice nominee, Senators can be expected to apply criteria which focus on the unique demands of that office, in addition to standards they might apply to Supreme Court nominees in general. This special focus was evident during the Senate's 1986 debate on the nomination of Associate Justice William H. Rehnquist to be Chief Justice. During the debate, various supporters and opponents of the nomination based their positions in significant part on standards they applied uniquely to a Chief Justice nominee. For instance, Senator Joseph R. Biden, Jr. (D-DE), who opposed the nomination, expressed concern as to "whether Justice Rehnquist can serve effectively as a leader of the Court, and to my mind this does not mean whether or not he can be an effective administrator, or whether or not he will do that expeditiously."[118] Senator Biden explained that he found Justice Rehnquist wanting, based on "two elements" of leadership that he thought necessary in a Chief Justice of the United States:

> One, a Chief Justice must exhibit the capability and willingness to work for and forge a consensus for unanimous opinions in watershed cases, cases where if there is not a unanimous decision there would be serious problems in this Nation.... Second, the Chief Justice must demonstrate the flexibility and open-mindedness to put aside his own philosophical or legal views when consensus on the Court is required even if he disagrees with the majority's holding.[119]

By contrast, Senator Orrin G. Hatch (R-UT), who supported the nominee, found that Justice Rehnquist more than measured up to the leadership qualities required in a Chief Justice:

> For over 15 years, Justice Rehnquist has earned a reputation as a leader amongst leaders on the nine-member Court. He knows better than perhaps anyone in the Nation the responsibility of serving as a 'keeper of the contract,' a protector of the agreement between the government and the governed. He, better than perhaps anyone in the Nation, can impart that vision in his fellow Federal judges throughout the Federal Judiciary. He already has the trust and respect of his peers and the rest of the bench and bar.[120]

## Voting on Both a Chief Justice and an Associate Justice Nomination

When the President selects a sitting Associate Justice to be Chief Justice and a nominee to succeed the elevated Associate Justice, two nominations will be transmitted to the Senate. If the President sends the nominations to the Senate at the same time, or within days of each other, the Senate can be expected —but is not required — to act on the Chief Justice nomination first.

Historically, there have been four episodes (three successful, one unsuccessful) in which Associate Justices were nominated to be Chief Justice and accompanying nominations were made to fill the positions of the elevated Associate Justices. In reverse chronological order, these involved the following nominations of Associate Justices to be Chief Justice: William H. Rehnquist in 1986, Abe Fortas in 1968, Harlan F. Stone in 1941, and Edward D. White in 1910. In a fifth, much earlier episode, another Associate Justice, William Cushing in 1796, was nominated, by President George Washington, to be Chief Justice, but Cushing's Chief Justice nomination to the Senate was unaccompanied by another nomination to fill the Associate Justice seat.

Most recently, in 1986, the Senate received President Ronald Reagan's nominations of William H. Rehnquist to be Chief Justice on June 20 and Antonin Scalia to be Associate Justice on June 24. On the same day, September 17, the Senate considered and voted to confirm Rehnquist and then considered and voted to confirm Scalia.[121] Prior to these Senate actions, the Senate Judiciary Committee held confirmation hearings first on Rehnquist, and then on Scalia, before favorably reporting both nominations to the Senate on the same day.

The previous instance in which a President tried (in this case, unsuccessfully) to use a Chief Justice vacancy to make two Court appointments involved President Lyndon B. Johnson. On June 26, 1968, President Johnson nominated both Associate Justice Abe Fortas to be Chief Justice and federal appellate court judge Homer Thornberry to be Associate Justice. The Senate Judiciary Committee held 11 days of confirmation hearings on the two nominations, focusing most of the time on the Fortas nomination. The committee then reported only the Fortas nomination to the Senate, declining to take further action on the Thornberry nomination while the outcome of the Fortas nomination was in doubt.[122] Subsequently, the Senate rejected a motion to close debate on a motion to proceed to consider the Fortas nomination, after which the Fortas and Thornberry nominations were both withdrawn by the President (the latter having advanced in committee only through the hearings stage).

In another two-appointment episode, however, the Senate acted on the Associate Justice nomination before the Chief Justice nomination. On June 12, 1941, President Franklin Delano Roosevelt nominated both Harlan F. Stone to be Chief Justice and Senator James F. Byrnes (D-SC) to succeed Justice Stone as Associate Justice. In keeping with a longstanding Senate practice of dispensing with confirmation hearings for a fellow Member,[123] the Senate confirmed the Byrnes nomination immediately on June 12, the day of its receipt by the Senate, without first referring it to committee. The nomination of Justice Stone to be Chief Justice took a longer route; it was confirmed almost two weeks later, on June 27, after confirmation hearings and being reported by the Judiciary Committee. Although the Senate had confirmed Senator Byrnes' nomination more quickly, his swearing-in as Associate Justice had to wait until the position was vacated by Justice Stone. Following his confirmation as Chief Justice on June 27, Justice Stone stepped down as Associate Justice on July 2 and took his judicial oath as Chief Justice on July 3, after which Associate Justice Byrnes was sworn in on July 8.

William Howard Taft was the first President to use a Chief Justice vacancy to make two Court appointments. On December 12, 1910, he sent to the Senate the nominations of both Associate Justice Edward D. White to be Chief Justice and of Willis Van Devanter to fill the position to be vacated by Justice White. In recognition of Justice White's service in the Senate prior to his appointment to the Court in 1894, the Senate immediately, by voice vote, confirmed him to be Chief Justice, declining to refer the nomination of their former Senate colleague to committee. Shortly thereafter, on December 15, the Van Devanter nomination was reported favorably by the Senate Judiciary Committee and, that same day, confirmed by the Senate by voice vote.

## Voice Votes, Roll Calls, and Vote Margins

When floor debate on a nomination comes to a close, the presiding officer puts the question of confirmation to a vote. In doing so, the presiding officer typically states, "The question is, Will the Senate advise and consent to the nomination of [nominee's name] of [nominee's state of residence] to be an Associate Justice [or Chief Justice] on the Supreme Court?" A vote to confirm requires a simple majority of Senators present and voting.

Since 1967, every Senate vote on whether to confirm a Supreme Court nomination has been by roll call.[124] Prior to 1967, by contrast, less than half of all of

Senate votes on whether to confirm nominees to the Court were by roll call, the rest by voice vote.[125] Of the 21 nominations made to the office of Chief Justice (from John Jay's nomination in 1789 to William H. Rehnquist's in 1986), 18 received Senate floor votes on the question of whether to confirm. All 18, except for one (the Senate's vote in 1795 vote rejecting the John Rutledge nomination), were in favor of confirmation. Of the 17 Chief Justice confirmations, 10 were by voice vote and seven by roll call.[126] The most recent voice vote on a Chief Justice nomination was the 1954 vote to confirm Earl Warren. Since then, the Chief Justice nominations of Warren E. Burger in 1969 and William H. Rehnquist were confirmed by roll call votes of 74-3 and 65-33 respectively. The three Chief Justice nominations which did not receive final Senate floor votes were, in the face of significant Senate opposition, withdrawn by the Presidents.[127]

Historically, vote margins on Supreme Court nominations have varied considerably. Some recorded votes, either confirming or rejecting a nomination, have been close.[128] Most votes, however, have been overwhelmingly in favor of confirmation.[129] The closest roll call votes involving Chief Justice nominations were the Senate's 14-10 rejection of the Rutledge nomination in 1795, the Senate's 25-19 vote in 1836 in favor of proceeding to the nomination of Roger B. Taney (which was followed by a 29-15 vote to confirm)[130] and the Senate's 45-43 vote in 1968 on a motion to close debate on a motion to proceed to the Abe Fortas nomination. (The vote on cloture fell short of the necessary super-majority to close debate, and three days later, the President, at Fortas's request, withdrew the nomination.)[131]

## Filibusters and Motions to Close Debate

Senate rules place no general limits on how long floor consideration of a nomination (or most other matters) may last. Without such time limits, Senators opposing a Supreme Court nominee may be able to use extended debate or other delaying actions to prevent a vote from occurring. The use of such dilatory actions is known as the filibuster.[132]

Since 1949, however, supporters of nominations which encountered extended debate on the Senate floor have had available to them a procedure for placing time limits on that debate — the motion for cloture.[133] When the Senate adopts a cloture motion, further consideration of the matter being filibustered is limited to 30 hours. By adopting a cloture motion, the Senate may be able to ensure that a nomination will ultimately come to a final vote and be decided by a voting majority. The majority currently required for cloture on most matters, including nominations, is three-fifths of the full membership of the Senate — normally 60 Senators.[134]

Cloture motions have been made in debate on Supreme Court nominations on only three occasions, two involving Chief Justice nominations. The first use occurred in 1968 during debate concerning the nomination of Associate Justice Abe Fortas to be Chief Justice. On September 24, 1968, Senate Majority Leader Mike

Mansfield (D-MT) called the Senate into executive session and moved that the Senate proceed to consider the nomination. Debate on that motion began the next day and continued on September 25, 26, 27, and 30, consuming more than 25 hours. On October 1, the Senate failed to invoke cloture, by a vote of 45 in favor and 43 opposed,[135] prompting President Lyndon B. Johnson to withdraw the nomination.[136] A detailed historical narrative of the Fortas nomination, published later in 1968, described the floor debate in opposition to Fortas, as a "filibuster intended to block confirmation of Justice Abe Fortas as Chief Justice of the United States."[137]

A cloture motion to end debate on a Court nomination occurred again in 1971, when the Senate considered the nomination of William H. Rehnquist to be an Associate Justice. Although the cloture motion failed by a 52-42 vote,[138] Rehnquist subsequently was confirmed. In 1986, a motion was filed to close debate on a third Supreme Court nomination, this time of sitting Justice Rehnquist to be Chief Justice. Supporters of the nomination mustered more than the three-fifths majority needed to close debate (with the Senate voting for cloture 68-31),[139] and Justice Rehnquist subsequently was confirmed as Chief Justice.

Although use of the filibuster against Supreme Court nominations has been relatively rare in the past, the number of filibusters conducted against lower court nominations has increased dramatically in recent years. During the 108th Congress, extended debate was successfully used in the Senate to block confirmation votes on 10 of President George W. Bush's 34 nominees to U.S. circuit court of appeals judgeships, and several of these nominations, after resubmission by President Bush in the 109th Congress, again faced the prospect of being filibustered by Senate Democrats. In response, in May of 2005, leaders of the Senate's Republican majority announced their intention, if filibusters against nominations continued, to amend the chamber's rules to require the vote of only a simple Senate majority to close Senate debate on judicial nominations.[140]

A Senate confrontation between the two parties over judicial filibusters was averted on May 23, 2005, when a compromise agreement was reached by a coalition of seven Democratic and seven Republican Senators. As part of the agreement, the coalition's Democratic Senators pledged not to lend their support to filibusters against judicial nominations except under "extraordinary circumstances," while the Republican Senators in the coalition agreed not to support any change in the Senate rules to bar filibusters against judicial nominations, as long as the "spirit and continuing commitments made in this agreement" were kept by all of Senators in the coalition.[141]

In recent years, some Senators have raised the possibility of a filibuster being conducted against a future Supreme Court nomination, particularly if a vacancy on the Court occurred during the presidency of George W. Bush.[142] In the current political climate, a filibuster against a nomination to the Court also could be regarded as a possibility, if a substantial number of Senators opposed a nominee's confirmation and viewed extended debate as a tactic that might succeed in blocking a Senate vote on confirmation from occurring. Such a strategy, however, would no longer be an option to opponents of the nominee if the Senate's rules, either prior to or during debate over the nomination, were modified to curtail use of filibusters against judicial nominations.[143]

# Chapter 4

# NOMINATION OF JOHN G. ROBERTS, JR.

On September 5, 2005, President George W. Bush announced he would nominate U.S. Court of Appeals Judge John G. Roberts, Jr., to succeed Chief Justice William H. Rehnquist, who had died two days earlier. The President cited Judge Roberts' "extraordinary career," his "striking ability as a lawyer and his natural gifts as a leader."[144] The death of Chief Justice Rehnquist, the President observed, "leaves the center chair empty just four weeks left before the Supreme Court reconvenes." It is "in the interest of the Court and the country," the President continued, "to have a chief justice on the bench on the first full day of the fall term."[145]

Judge Roberts had been nominated by President Bush earlier, on July 29, 2005, to succeed retiring Associate Justice Sandra Day O'Connor.[146] Five weeks later, the pre-hearings phase for that nomination was approaching its end,[147] with the Senate Judiciary Committee set to begin confirmation hearings for Judge Roberts on September 6, the first day of the Senate's return from its August recess.

The death of Chief Justice Rehnquist on September 3, 2005, however, dramatically transformed the appointments equation for the Supreme Court, the President and the Senate. As a result of the Chief Justice's passing, there were now two vacancies — an immediate Chief Justice vacancy, and a prospective vacancy with the announced intention of Justice O'Connor to retire upon the confirmation of her successor. For President Bush, the Rehnquist vacancy provided a new opportunity, if the President wished — to appoint Judge Roberts to a different seat on the Court. In this vein, a newspaper reported in its September 5 morning editions that Judge Roberts was now being considered by the Bush White House for nomination to be Chief Justice:

The idea of making Roberts chief justice seems to have natural appeal. Roberts, a former lawyer in the Ronald Reagan and George H.W. Bush administrations who now serves as a judge on the U.S. Court of Appeals for the District of Columbia Circuit, was first interviewed by the White House in April not for O'Connor's seat but in the expectation that Rehnquist would retire or die.

As a former Rehnquist clerk, Roberts could be expected to continue in the same conservative course, and at 50 he would have a long tenure in the top slot. After six weeks of media scrutiny, he is also a known commodity who has not generated strong opposition among Senate Democrats.

The mechanics of a switch would not be hard. Bush would withdraw Roberts's nomination as associate justice and then simultaneously nominate him as chief justice. Bush could then take his time choosing someone else to replace O'Connor because she has agreed to remain on the court until her successor's confirmation.[148]

Indeed, the very morning on which the above news report appeared, President Bush would announce his selection of Judge Roberts to be Chief Justice. In doing so, the President also emphasized that, from his perspective, the Senate was "well along in the process of considering Judge Roberts' qualifications."[149] The next day, September 6, the Chairman of the Judiciary Committee, the committee's Ranking Democratic Member, and Senate leaders announced a new schedule for Judge Roberts' confirming hearings, this time as nominee to be Chief Justice — with hearings to begin on September 12, 2005.

In the days ahead, Chief Justice nominee Roberts will be closely examined first by the Senate Judiciary Committee and then by the Senate as a whole. Consistent with the nature of questioning directed at Court nominees during confirmation hearings in the 1980s and 1990s, Senators' questioning of Judge Roberts, at his confirmation hearings, can be expected to be rigorous and to cover a wide range of subject areas.[150] Following the hearings, the Judiciary Committee, in keeping with long-established practice, can be expected to report the nomination to the Senate floor, regardless of the breakdown of votes in favor of or opposed to confirmation.

For more than a century, the tradition of the Senate has been that the question of whether to confirm Supreme Court nominees is not decided in the committee stage, but by the Senate as a whole.

Senators will evaluate Judge Roberts' fitness to be Chief Justice according to their own criteria and concerns. In large part, however, their concerns will mirror the traditional concerns of Presidents with professional excellence, character, and leadership qualities in a Chief Justice nominee. Senators also may be concerned with the nominee's judicial philosophy or views on constitutional issues and how, in their view, the appointment might affect the Court's future direction on major legal and constitutional questions.

It has been suggested, as noted earlier, that if a Supreme Court nominee were to prove controversial, a filibuster against the nomination would be a possibility, unless Senate rules were modified to curtail the use of filibusters against judicial nominees. Under current Senate rules, the nomination would fall short of confirmation if, in the event of a filibuster, three-fifths of the Senate's full membership failed to vote in favor of closing debate. As also noted earlier, an agreement reached on May 23, 2005, by a coalition of seven Democratic and seven Republican Senators averted what until then had seemed an imminent confrontation between the two parties over judicial filibusters. As part of that agreement, the coalition's Democratic Senators pledged not to lend their support to filibusters against judicial nominations except under "extraordinary circumstances."

If and when the Senate votes to close debate on the Chief Justice nomination, the next and ultimate test for appointment will be the Senate vote on whether to confirm. A vote to confirm would require a simple majority of Senators present and voting. If the vote of the majority is to confirm, the confirmed nominee would then receive a commission from the President, officially appointing him to the Court. After receiving his commission, Judge Roberts would be sworn into office, becoming the 17th Chief Justice of the United States.

# Table 1. Nominees for Chief Justice of the United States, 1789 to the Present: Dates of Nomination, Final Action by the Senate or President, Judicial Oath and Termination of Service, and Ages at Times of Appointment and Termination of Service

| Nominee (and State) | President | Nomination Date | Final Action(s) by Senate or President | | Judicial Oath Taken | | Termination of Service | | |
|---|---|---|---|---|---|---|---|---|---|
| | | | Date | Action | Date | Age | Date | Reason | Age |
| John Jay (New York) | Washington | 09/24/1789 | 09/26/1789 | Confirmed, voice vote | 10/19/1789 | 44 | 06/29/1795 | Resigned | 49 |
| *John Rutledge* (South Carolina) | Washington | | Recess appointment, 07/01/1795 | | 08/12/1795 | 55 | 12/28/1795 | Resigned | 56 |
| | | 12/10/1795 | 12/15/1795 | Rejected, 10-14 | — | | — | | |
| **William Cushing** (Massachusetts) | Washington | 01/26/1796 | 01/27/1796 | Confirmed, voice vote; Nominee declined | — | | — | | |
| Oliver Ellsworth (Connecticut) | Washington | 03/03/1796 | 03/04/1796 | Confirmed, 21-1 | 03/08/1796 | 50 | 12/15/1800 | Resigned | 55 |
| *John Jay* (New York) | Adams, John | 12/18/1800 | 12/19/1800 | Confirmed, voice vote; Nominee declined | — | | — | | |
| John Marshall (Virginia) | Adams, John | 01/20/1801 | 01/27/1801 | Confirmed, voice vote | 02/04/1801 | 45 | 07/06/1835 | Died in Office | 79 |
| Roger Brooke Taney (Maryland) | Jackson | 12/28/1835 | 03/14/1836; 03/15/1836 | Proceed, 25-19; Confirmed, 29-15 | 03/28/1836 | 59 | 10/12/1864 | Died in Office | 87 |
| Salmon P. Chase (Ohio) | Lincoln | 12/06/1864 | 12/06/1864 | Confirmed, voice vote | 12/15/1864 | 56 | 05/07/1873 | Died in Office | 65 |

Table 1. (Continued)

| Nominee (and State) | President | Nomination Date | Final Action(s) by Senate or President | | Judicial Oath Taken | | Termination of Service | | |
|---|---|---|---|---|---|---|---|---|---|
| | | | Date | Action | Date | Age | Date | Reason | Age |
| George H. Williams (Oregon) | Grant | 12/02/1873 | 12/15/1873 | Recommitted | — | | — | | |
| Caleb Cushing (Massachusetts) | Grant | 01/09/1874 | 01/08/1874 | Withdrawn | | | | | |
| | | | 01/13/1874 | Withdrawn | — | | — | | |
| Morrison R. Waite(Ohio) | Grant | 01/19/1874 | 01/21/1874 | Confirmed, 63-0 | 03/04/1874 | 57 | 03/23/1888 | Died in Office | 71 |
| Melville W. Fuller(Illinois) | Cleveland | 05/02/1888 | 07/20/1888 | Confirmed, 41-20 | 10/08/1888 | 55 | 07/04/1910 | Died in Office | 77 |
| Edward D. White(Louisiana) | Taft | 12/12/1910 | 12/12/1910 | Confirmed, voice vote | 12/19/1910 | 65 | 05/19/1921 | Died in Office | 75 |
| William Howard Taft(Connecticut) | Harding | 06/30/1921 | 06/30/1921 | Confirmed, voice vote | 07/11/1921 | 63 | 02/03/1930 | Retired | 72 |
| Charles Evans Hughes (New York) | Hoover | 02/03/1930 | 02/13/1930 | Recommit, 31-49 | 02/24/1930 | 67 | 06/30/1941 | Retired | 79 |
| | | | | Confirmed, 51-26 | | | | | |
| Harlan Fiske Stone (New York) | Roosevelt, F. | 06/12/1941 | 06/27/1941 | Confirmed, voice vote | 07/03/1941 | 68 | 04/22/1946 | Died in Office | 73 |
| Fred M. Vinson(Kentucky) | Truman | 06/06/1946 | 06/20/1946 | Confirmed, voice vote | 06/24/1946 | 56 | 09/08/1953 | Died in Office | 63 |

# Table 1. (Continued)

| Nominee (and State) | President | Nomination Date | Final Action(s) by Senate or President | | Judicial Oath Taken | | Termination of Service | | |
|---|---|---|---|---|---|---|---|---|---|
| | | | Date | Action | Date | Age | Date | Reason | Age |
| Earl Warren (California) | Eisenhower | *Recess appointment, 10/02/1953* | | | 10/05/1953 | | — | Retired | 78 |
| | | 01/11/1954 | 03/01/1954 | Confirmed, voice vote | — | 62 | 06/23/1969 | — | |
| Abe Fortas (Tennessee) | Johnson | 06/28/1968 | 10/01/1968 | Cloture, 45-43 | | | — | | |
| | | | 10/04/1968 | Withdrawn | — | | | | |
| Warren E. Burger (Virginia) | Nixon | 05/23/1969 | 06/09/1969 | Confirmed, 74-3 | 06/23/1969 | 61 | 06/26/1986 | Resigned | 79 |
| **William H. Rehnquist** (Virginia) | Reagan | 07/20/1986 | 09/17/1986 | Cloture, 68-31 | 09/26/1986 | 61 | 09/03/2005 | Died in office | 80 |
| | | | | Confirmed, 65-33 | | | | | |
| **John G. Roberts, Jr.** (Virgina) | Bush, George W. | 09/06/2005 | Nomination pending | | | | | | |

**Legend: Name in Bold** — Was serving as Associate Justice at time of nomination to be Chief Justice.

*Name in Italics* — Had earlier served as Associate Justice, prior to, but not at, time of nomination to be Chief Justice. ***Name in Bold Italics*** — Had earlier served as Chief Justice.

**Sources:** William D. Bader and Roy M. Mersky, *The First One Hundred Justices*, (Buffalo: William S. Hein & Co., Inc., 2004 ); Artemus Ward, *Deciding to Leave*, (Albany: State University of New York Press, 2003); *Journal of the Executive Proceedings of the Senate of the United States of America* (various volumes); *The Supreme Court of the United States* (an undated pamphlet published by the United States Supreme Court); and Maeva Marcus and James R. Perry, editors, *The Documentary History of the Supreme Court of the United States, 1789-1800* (New York: Columbia University Press, 1985).

# REFERENCES

[1]    Three of the Chief Justices each served more than 20 years — John Marshall, 34 years (from 1801 to 1935), Roger Brooke Taney, 28½ years (from 1836 to 1864), and Melville Fuller, 22 years (from 1888 to 1910).

[2]    Already an Associate Justice at the time, William H. Rehnquist was nominated to be Chief Justice on July 20, 1986, was confirmed by the Senate on Sept. 17, 1986, and took his judicial oath as Chief Justice nine days later. After taking his oath of office as an Associate Justice on Jan. 7, 1972, Rehnquist served on the Court for almost 34 years.

[3]    Justice O'Connor, in a July 1, 2005 letter, informed President George W. Bush of her decision to retire from the Court "effective upon the nomination and confirmation of my successor." Sandra Day O'Connor, letter to President George W. Bush, July 1, 2005, available at *[http://www.supremecourtus.gov/publicinfo/press/pr_07-0105.html].*

[4]    President Bush's announcement of his intention to nominate Judge Roberts to be Chief Justice came on Sept. 5, 2005. The next day, the actual nomination document was signed and sent to the Senate, and the nomination of Judge Roberts to be Associate Justice was withdrawn . See "President Nominates Judge Roberts to be Supreme Court Chief Justice," Sept. 5, 2005 White House News release, including text of the nomination announcement, available at *[http://www.whitehouse.gov/news/releases/2005/09/print/200 50905.html].*

[5]    Only three Chief Justices were 50 years of age or younger when they were sworn into office: John Jay, who was 44 when he became the nation's first Chief Justice in 1789; Oliver Ellsworth, who was 50 upon becoming the third Chief Justice in 1796; and John Marshall, who was 45 when he became the fourth Chief Justice in 1801. When

Ellsworth took his judicial oath of office on March 8, 1796, he was less than two months away from his 51st birthday. Hence, if confirmed by the Senate and sworn into office before mid-November 2005, Judge Roberts, who was born on Jan. 27, 1955, would become the third youngest person ever to serve as Chief Justice.

[6]    See, for example, Sen. Patrick J. Leahy, remarks in the Senate, *Congressional Record*, daily ed., vol. 150, Nov. 20, 2004, pp. S11830-S11832.

[7]    See, for example, speech by Sen. William H. Frist delivered on Nov. 11, 2004, to the Federalist Society, in *Congressional Record*, daily ed., vol. 150, Nov. 24, 2004, pp. S11848-S11849. See also the historic debate of almost 40 consecutive hours between Senate Republicans and Senate Democrats (from evening of Nov. 12 to the morning of Nov. 14, 2003) on the propriety of filibusters against judicial nominations, and on related judicial nominations issues, in *Congressional Record*, daily ed., vol. 149, Nov. 12, 2003, pp. S14528-S14790.

[8]    A journalist covering the Supreme Court in 2001 noted that announcements by the Court of 5-4 decisions had "become routine, a familiar reminder of how much the next appointment to the court will matter." Linda Greenhouse, "Divided They Stand: The High Court and the Triumph of Discord," *New York Times,* July 15, 2001, sec. 4, p. 1.

[9]    Subsequently, the number of Associate Justice seats on the Court has been increased or decreased legislatively by Congress on five separate occasions. From 1869 to the present, though, the number of Justice seats on the Court has been fixed at nine.

[10]   David G. Savage, *Guide to the U.S. Supreme Court*, 4th ed., vol. 2 (Washington: CQ Press, 2004), pp. 867-869.

[11]   See John J. Patrick, *The Supreme Court of the United States: A Student Companion*, 2nd ed. (New York: Oxford University Press, 2001), p. 70.

[12]   Since the mid-1970s, the Supreme Court Clerk's records have been computerized. In April 2000, the Supreme Court's website, at [http://www.supremecourtus.gov], brought the Court into the age of electronic information. Attendant to these technological advances are administrative and budgetary demands, as well as heightened expectations that extensive and timely Court-related information will be accessible to the public. Among the 400 people who work in the Supreme Court building are the key officers who carry out the

Court's statutory duties: the Clerk, the Library, the Marshal, and the reporter of Decisions. Visitors and tourists to the Court now exceed one million annually. Since the terrorist attack of Sept. 11, 2001, and the anthrax threat, increased physical security for the Court, its employees, and visitors also has been a concern. Overseeing all of these matters is now an integral part of the Chief Justice's responsibilities. In 1972 Congress authorized the Chief Justice to employ an administrative assistant to perform duties as assigned by the Chief Justice. The Chief is also authorized to have the services of up to four law clerks, three secretaries, a messenger, and a government car and driver.

[13] 28 U.S.C. § 331. The Judicial Conference of the United States is the policy-making body for the administration of the federal court system. The conference comprises the chief judges of the 13 courts of appeals, a district court judge from each of the 12 regional circuits, and the chief judge of the Court of International Trade. For more information, see [http://www.uscourts.gov/judconf.html].

[14] 28 U.S.C. § 601. The Administrative Office of the United States Courts is the central administrative and budgetary support agency for the federal court system.

[15] 28 U.S.C. § 621. The Federal Judicial Center is a support agency for the federal judiciary, which, through research and training programs for judges and judicial personnel, seeks to further improvements in judicial administration.

[16] Associated Press, "Attn.: John Roberts," *Washington Post*, Sept. 7, 2005, p. A23.

[17] Available at [http://www.uscourts.gov/ttb/jan05ttb/].

[18] Typically, the annual report summarizes events of the federal judiciary over the past year (including the work of the Supreme Court, the Federal Judicial Center, the Administrative Office of the United States Courts, and the United States Sentencing Commission). It also highlights legislative developments bearing directly on the federal judiciary and provides statistics on the federal court caseload over the past year.

[19] 28 U.S.C. § 42. By statute, a justice may be assigned to more than one circuit, and two or more justices may be assigned to the same circuit. A listing of the Associate Justices' allotment to the circuits, as of September 7, 2005, is available at [http://www.supremecourtus.gov/about/090705pzr.pdf].

[20] 28 U.S.C. § 291(a).

[21]   28 U.S.C. § 294(a). The chief judge or circuit justice of the circuit where the need arises must present a certificate of necessity to the Chief Justice for such designation or assignment to a court of appeals or district court. The statute also explicitly states that, "No such designation or assignment shall be made to the Supreme Court."

[22]   20 U.S.C. § 42.

[23]   20 U.S.C. § 72.

[24]   20 U.S.C. § 76cc.

[25]   18 U.S.C.A. prec. § note.

[26]   44 U.S.C. § 2501.

[27]   Technically, the oath of office may be administered by any judge.

[28]   The *2001 Year-End Report on the Federal Judiciary* noted that the Chief Justice led a delegation representing the federal judiciary to Mexico at the invitation of the the the President of the Mexican Supreme Court as part of a judicial exchange (a follow-up to a similar visit by a Mexican delegation to Washington in 1999). In 2001, more than 800 representatives from over 40 federal judicial systems around the world visited the Supreme Court to learn about the American judicial system.

[29]   28 U.S.C. § 3.

[30]   William H. Rehnquist, Remarks of The Chief Justice on My Life in the Law Series, Duke University School of Law, April 13, 2002, available at *[http://www.supremecourtus.gov/publicinfo/speeches/ sp_04-14-03.html]*. In Latin, primus means first and pares means equals.

[31]   There are no constitutional provisions setting forth professional qualifications for federal judges in general, nor do any statutes set forth professional qualifications for federal judges with lifetime appointments. (Judges with lifetime appointments include the Supreme Court's Justices and judges on the U.S. district courts, the U.S. courts of appeals, and the U.S. Court of International Trade). "The very few statutory professional prerequisites apply only to nominees to federal courts whose judges are not constitutionally entitled to 'good Behaviour' [i.e., lifetime] tenure." CRS Report 95-404A, *Professional Qualifications for Appointment to the Federal Judiciary,* by P. L. Morgan (archived; available from D. Steven Rutkus).

[32]   For discussion of the past role of the ABA Standing Committee in evaluating and rating the qualifications of Supreme Court nominees for the benefit of Presidents and the Senate Judiciary Committee, see

CRS Report RL31989, *Supreme Court Appointment Process*, pp. 12-13 and pp. 20-22. See also CRS Report 96-446 GOV, *The American Bar Association's Standing Committee on Federal Judiciary: A Historical Overview,* by Denis Steven Rutkus (archived; available from the author).

[33]   *The ABA Standing Committee on Federal Judiciary: What It Is and How It Works*, American Bar Association, available at *[http://www. abanet.org/scfedjud/backgrounder. html]*.

[34]   Ibid. The criterion of integrity, the committee booklet explains, concerns "the nominee's character and general reputation in the legal community," as well as "his or her industry and diligence." Judicial temperament involves "the prospective nominee's compassion, decisiveness, open-mindedness, courtesy, patience, freedom from bias, and commitment to equal justice under the law."

[35]   Ibid.

[36]   Only four Associate Justices were, at the time they were serving on the Court, nominated to be Chief Justice — Edward D. White in 1910, Harlan Fiske Stone in 1941, Abe Fortas in 1968, and William H. Rehnquist in 1986. (White, Stone, and Rehnquist received Senate confirmation to be Chief Justice, but Fortas did not.) Two others appointed to be Chief Justice, John Rutledge in 1795 and Charles Evans Hughes in 1930, had earlier served as Associate Justices, but were not serving on the Court at the time of their Chief Justice appointments.

[37]   John Paul Frank, *Marble Palace; the Supreme Court in American Life* (Westport, CT: Greenwood Press,1972), pp. 78-79.

[38]   Charles Evans Hughes, *The Supreme Court of the United States* (New York: Columbia University Press, 1928), p. 57.

[39]   Frankfurter, quoted by James Reston, in "Choice of New Chief Justice Could Hinge on Many Tests," *New York Times*, Sept. 10, 1953, p. 20.

[40]   See also CRS General Distribution Memorandum, *Criteria Used by Senators to Evaluate Judicial Nominations*, by Denis Steven Rutkus (available from the author), for a discussion of the wide range of criteria that Senators have been understood to use in deciding whether to vote to confirm nominees for federal judgeships.

[41]   For a more complete review of each stage of the Supreme Court appointment process, as its applies to Associate Justice as well as Chief Justice nominees, see CRS Report RL31989, *Supreme Court*

*Appointment Process: Roles of the President, Judiciary Committee, and Senate,* by Denis Steven Rutkus.

[42]    An incoming Justice takes two oaths of office — a judicial oath, as required by the Judiciary Act of 1789, and a constitutional oath, which, as required by Article VI of the U.S. Constitution, is administered to Members of Congress and all executive and judicial officers. In 1986, both oaths of office were administered to incoming Chief Justice William H. Rehnquist by retiring Chief Justice Warren E. Burger — the constitutional oath at the White House, the judicial oath at the Supreme Court. In 1969 both oaths were administered at the Supreme Court to incoming Chief Justice Burger by retiring Chief Justice Earl Warren. In 1953, both oaths were administered to incoming Chief Justice Warren at the Supreme Court — the constitutional oath by the senior Associate Justice in point of service, Hugo L. Black, and the judicial oath by the Clerk of the Court, Harold B. Willey. See Ruth Marcus, "Rehnquist, Scalia Take Their Oaths," *Washington Post*, Sept. 27, 1986, p. A14; "Burger is Sworn as Chief Justice," *New York Times*, June 24, 1969, p.1; and "Warren Takes Place on Bench as High Court Meets Today," *Washington Post*, Oct. 5, 1953, p. 1.

[43]    See Table 1 at end of this report, which lists the names of all past Chief Justice nominees chronologically by the dates of their nominations. The table, among other things, indicates which nominees received Senate confirmation, which had prior service on the Court (either as an Associate Justice or, in one instance, as Chief Justice), and which two declined their appointments after being confirmed.

[44]    See the 1795 appointment of John Rutledge, in Table 1 at the end of this report.

[45]    See, in Table 1 at the end of this report, the nominations of George H. Williams in 1873, Caleb Cushing in 1874, and Abe Fortas in 1968.

[46]    See 1800 nomination of Jay in Table 1, at the end of this report. For text of Jan. 2, 1801, letter from John Jay to President John Adams, declining the appointment, see Maeva Marcus et al., eds., *The Documentary History of the Supreme Court of the United States, 1789-1800*, vol. 1, part 1 ("Appointments and Proceedings") (New York: Columbia University Press, 1985), pp. 146-147. (Hereafter cited as Marcus, *Documentary History*.)

[47]    See, at the end of this report, the 1796 nomination of Associate Justice William Cushing to be Chief Justice. For text of Feb. 2, 1796,

letter of Justice Cushing to President George Washington, declining the Chief Justice appointment, see Marcus, *Documentary History*, pp. 103-104.

[48]   U.S. Constitution, Article III, Section 1.

[49]   Ibid. Article III, Section 1, provides, in part, that the "judicial Power of the United States, shall be vested in one supreme Court, and in such inferior Courts as the Congress may from time to time ordain and establish. The Judges, both of the supreme and inferior courts, shall hold their offices during good Behaviour...." In the present federal court system, the courts established by Congress under Article III, Section 1, whose judgeships entail lifetime appointments, are the U.S. District Courts, the U.S. Courts of Appeals, and the U.S. Court of International Trade.

[50]   Alexander Hamilton, in Federalist Paper 78 ("The Judges as Guardians of the Constitution"), maintained that while the judiciary was "in continual jeopardy of being overpowered, awed, or influenced by its coordinate branches ... , nothing can contribute so much to its firmness and independence as *permanency in office*." He added that if the courts "are to be considered as the bulwarks of a limited Constitution against legislative encroachments, this consideration will afford a strong argument for the *permanent tenure* of judicial offices, since *nothing will contribute so much as this to that independent spirit in the judges*...." (emphases added). Benjamin Fletcher Wright, ed., *The Federalist by Alexander Hamilton, James Madison, and John Jay* (Cambridge, MA: Belknap Press of Harvard University Press, 1966), pp. 491 (first quote) and 494 (second quote). (Hereafter cited as Wright, *The Federalist*.)

[51]   In 1804 the House of Representatives voted to impeach Justice Samuel Chase. The vote to impeach Chase, a staunch Federalist and outspoken critic of Jeffersonian Republican policies, was strictly along party lines. In 1805, after a Senate trial, Chase was acquitted after votes in the Senate fell short of the necessary two-thirds majority on any of the impeachment articles approved by the House. "Chase's impeachment and trial set a precedent of strict construction of the impeachment clause and bolstered the judiciary's claim of independence from political tampering." Elder Witt, ed., *Congressional Quarterly's Guide to the U.S. Supreme Court*, 2nd ed. (Washington: Congressional Quarterly Inc, 1990), p. 235.

[52]   The decision of the framers of the Constitutional Convention of 1787 to have the President and the Senate share in the appointment of the

Supreme Court Justices and other principal officers of the government, one scholar writes, was a compromise reached between "one group of men [who] feared the abuse of the appointing power by the executive and favored appointments by the legislative body," and "another group of more resolute men, eager to establish a strong national government with a vigorous administration, [who] favored the granting of the power of appointment to the President." Joseph P. Harris, *The Advice and Consent of the Senate: A Study of the Confirmation of Appointments by the United States Senate* (Berkeley: University of California Press, 1953; reprint, New York: Greenwood Press, 1968), p. 33. (Hereafter cited as Harris, *Advice and Consent.*)

[53]  Of the 15 persons who served as Chief Justice prior to the current office holder, three (specifically the first three) resigned, eight died in office, and four retired. Prior to 1869, there was no statutory retirement provision for Supreme Court Justices, and the departure mode for every Justice, Associate as well as Chief, was either death in office or resignation (with many Justices, for financial concerns, unable to afford to resign). Six consecutive Chief Justices (whose total service spanned the years 1801 to 1921) died in office. The first of four Chief Justices to retire, and thereby receive a government pension for his service, was William Howard Taft, in 1930. For a book-length examination of the considerations that Justices have weighed in deciding whether to resign or retire from the Court, see Artemus Ward, *Deciding To Leave: The Politics of Retirement from the United States Supreme Court* (Albany, NY: State University of New York Press, 2003). (Hereafter cited as Ward, *Deciding to Leave.*)

[54]  The four Chief Justices who retired from the Court were William Howard Taft, Charles Evans Hughes, Earl Warren, and Warren Burger. In a letter to President Herbert Hoover, dated Feb. 3, 1930, Chief Justice Taft stated that he was "desirous of accepting" the retirement benefits accorded to federal judges who had served as judges for at least 10 years and had attained the age of 70, and noted that his resignation was "intended to take effect immediately upon its acceptance by you." U.S. President (Hoover), "Letter Accepting the Resignation of William Howard Taft as Chief Justice of the Supreme Court,"*Public Papers of the Presidents of the United States — Herbert Hoover, 1930* (Washington: GPO, 1976), p. 42. Citing "considerations of health and age," Chief Justice Charles Evans Hughes in a letter to President Franklin D. Roosevelt, dated June 2,

1941, stated his intention to retire effective July 1, 1941. U.S. President (Roosevelt, F.), "Exchange of Communications Between the President and Chief Justice Charles Evans Hughes on His Retirement. June 2, 1941," *The Public Papers and Addresses of Franklin D. Roosevelt*, 1941 vol. (New York, Harper & Brothers, 1950), p. 200. In a June 13, 1968, letter to President Lyndon Johnson, Chief Justice Earl Warren declared his intention to retire as Chief Justice "effective at your pleasure." U.S. President (Johnson, L.), "The President's News Conference of June 26, 1968," *Public Papers of the Presidents of the United States — Lyndon B. Johnson,* 1968-69 volume, book 1 (Washington: GPO, 1970), p. 746. Because Warren did not specify a retirement date, the Johnson administration "interpreted it to mean that Warren would wait until a successor was confirmed." Ward, *Deciding to Leave*, p. 172. In early October 1968, after President Johnson's nomination of Associate Justice Abe Fortas to succeed Warren failed to gain Senate confirmation, Warren informed President Johnson that he would continue serving as Chief until a successor was confirmed. Johnson, for his part, declared he would not submit another Chief Justice nomination before leaving office in January 1969, leaving the Court vacancy to be filled by the person elected President in the November 1968 elections. U.S. President (Johnson, L.), "Statement by the President Upon Declining to Submit an Additional Nomination for the Office of Chief Justice of the United States. October 10, 1968," *Public Papers of the Presidents of the United States — Lyndon B. Johnson,* 1968-69 volume, book 1 (Washington: GPO, 1970), p. 1024. After taking office in January 1969, the newly elected President, Richard M. Nixon, "worked out a deal that allowed the Chief to finish out the 1968 Term before stepping down." Ward, *Deciding to Leave,* p. 174. In a letter to President Ronald Reagan, released by the White House on June 17, 1986, Chief Justice Burger asked to be relieved as Chief Justice "effective July 10, 1986, or as soon thereafter as my successor is qualified, pursuant to 28 U.S.C. §371(b)." U.S. President (Reagan), "Exchange of Letters on the Resignation of Warren E. Burger as Chief Justice. June 17, 1986," *Weekly Compilation of Presidential Documents*, vol. 22, June 23, 1986, p. 812.

[55] See discussion of the Rutledge recess appointment in later section of this report, under heading "Recess Appointments to the Court."

[56] 28 U.S.C. §372(b) addresses situations where U.S. district and U.S. circuit court of appeals judges are eligible to retire because of

permanent disability but decline to do so. In these cases, a certificate of disability may be signed by a majority of the members of the Judicial Council of the judge's circuit and presented to the President. If the President finds that the judge is "unable to discharge efficiently all the duties of his office by reason of permanent mental or physical disability and that the appointment of an additional judge is necessary for the efficient dispatch of business, the President may make such appointment by and with the advice and consent of the Senate." The President's appointment, in this situation, is not made to a vacated judgeship, but to a newly created judgeship (which temporarily increases by one the number of judges in the district or circuit). The judgeship of the permanently disabled judge becomes vacant only upon his or her death, resignation, or retirement. When that occurs, the statute provides that the vacancy shall not be refilled (causing the number of judgeships in the district or circuit to be reduced by one, reverting to the number of judgeships permanently authorized for the district or circuit).

[57]    28 U.S.C. §372 (a) provides that a Justice or lower federal court judge with lifetime tenure "who becomes permanently disabled from performing his duties may retire from regular active service," by certifying this disability to the President in writing. The Justice or judge who retires under this section, after 10 years of service, receives during the remainder of his or her lifetime the office's full salary, or one-half the salary of the office if having served less than 10 years.

[58]    Robert S. Greenberger, "On High Court, No Law Governs Quitting Time," *Wall Street Journal*, Dec. 28, 2004, p. A4.

[59]    George L. Watson and John A. Stookey, *Shaping America: the Politics of Supreme Court Appointments* (New York: Harper Collins College Publishers, 1995), pp. 58-59. (Hereafter cited as Watson and Stookey, *Shaping America.)*

[60]    Considerations of geographic representation, for example, influenced President George Washington, in 1789, to divide his first six appointments to the Court between three nominees from the North and three from the South. See Watson and Stookey, *Shaping America,* p. 60, and Henry J. Abraham, *Justices, Presidents, and Senators: A History of the U.S. Supreme Court Appointments from Washington to Clinton* (Lanham, MD: Rowman & Littlefield Publishers, Inc., 1999), pp. 59-60. (Hereafter cited as Abraham, *Justices, Presidents, and Senators.)* President Ronald Reagan in 1981, for example, was

sensitive to the absence of any female Justices on the Court. In announcing his choice of Sandra Day O'Connor to replace retiring Justice Potter Stewart, President Reagan noted that "during my campaign for the Presidency, I made a commitment that one of my first appointments to the Supreme Court vacancy would be the most qualified woman that I could possibly find." U.S. President (Reagan), "Remarks Announcing the Intention to Nominate Sandra Day O'Connor to Be an Associate Justice of the Supreme Court of the United States, July 7, 1981," *Public Papers of the Presidents of the United States, Ronald Reagan, 1981* (Washington: GPO, 1982), p. 596

[61]    While the "desire to appoint justices sympathetic to their own ideological and policy views may drive most presidents in selecting judges," the field of potentially acceptable nominees for most presidents, according to Watson and Stookey, is narrowed down by at least five "subsidiary motivations" — (1) rewarding personal or political support, (2) representing certain interests, (3) cultivating political support, (4) ensuring a safe nominee, and (5) picking the most qualified nominee. Watson and Stookey, *Shaping America*, p. 59.

[62]    One of the "unwritten codes," two scholars on the judiciary have written, "is that a judicial appointment is different from run-of-the-mill patronage. Thus, although the political rules may allow a president to reward an old ally with a seat on the bench, even here tradition has created an expectation that the would-be judge have some reputation for professional competence, the more so as the judgeship in question goes from the trial court to the appeals court to the Supreme Court level." Robert A. Carp and Ronald A. Stidham, *Judicial Process in America*, 3rd ed. (Washington: CQ Press, 1996), pp. 240-241.

[63]    President Gerald R. Ford, for example, said he believed his nominee, U.S. appellate court judge John Paul Stevens, "to be best qualified to serve as an Associate Justice of the Supreme Court." U.S. President (Ford), "Remarks Announcing Intention to Nominate John Paul Stevens to Be an Associate Justice of the Supreme Court, November 28, 1975," *Public Papers of the Presidents of the United States; Gerald R. Ford; 1975*, Book II (Washington: GPO, 1977), p. 1917. Similarly, in 1991, President George H. W. Bush said of nominee Clarence Thomas, "I believe he'll be a great justice. He is the best person for this position." U.S. President (Bush, George H. W.), "The

President's News Conference in Kennebunkport, Maine, July 1, 1991," *Public Papers of the President of the United State*s; *George Bush; 1991*, Book II (Washington: GPO, 1992), p. 801.

[64]  In Federalist Paper 78 ("Judges as Guardians of the Constitution"), Hamilton extolled the "benefits of the integrity and moderation of the Judiciary," which, he said, commanded "the esteem and applause of all the virtuous and disinterested." Further, he maintained, there could "be but few men" in society who would "unite the requisite integrity with the requisite knowledge" to "qualify them for the stations of judges." Wright, *The Federalist,* pp. 495 (first quote) and 496 (second quote).

[65]  James Reston, "Choice of New Chief Justice Could Hinge on Many Tests," *New York Times*, Sept. 10, 1953, p. 20.

[66]  Ibid.

[67]  Abraham, *Justices, Presidents, and Senators*, p. 192.

[68]  In his memoirs, President Eisenhower recounted that, a few months prior to the death of Chief Justice Vinson, he had talked to Governor Warren "about his basic philosophy and been quite pleased that his views seemed to reflect high ideals and a great deal of common sense. During this conversation I told the Governor that I was considering the possibility of appointing him to the Supreme Court and I was definitely inclined to do so if, in the future, a vacancy should occur." Dwight D. Eisenhower, *The White House Years,* 2 vols. (Garden City, NY: Doubleday & Company, Inc., 1963-65), vol. 1, p. 228.

[69]  Ibid., p.227.

[70]  Ibid., pp. 226-227.

[71]  Ibid., p. 226.

[72]  Ibid., p. 227.

[73]  Ibid., pp. 227-228.

[74]  Ibid., p. 230.

[75]  Immediately prior to their appointments to the Court, John M. Harlan (1955), Charles E. Whittaker (1957) and Potter Stewart (1958) had been U.S. circuit court of appeals judges, and William J. Brennan (1956) had been a state supreme court justice.

[76]  "To a certain extent, presidents have always looked to the Senate for recommendations and subsequently relied on a nominee's backers there to help move the nomination through the Senate." Watson and Stookey, *Shaping America,* p. 78.

[77]  President William Clinton's search for a successor to retiring Justice Harry A. Blackmun, during the spring of 1994, is illustrative of a

President seeking and receiving Senate advice. According to one report, the President, as he came close to a decision after holding his options "close to the vest" for more than a month, "began for the first time to consult with leading senators about his top candidates for the Court seat and solicited advice about prospects for easy confirmation." The advice he received included "sharp Republican opposition to one of his leading choices, Interior Secretary Bruce Babbitt." Gwen Ifill, "Clinton Again Puts Off Decision on Nominee for Court," *The New York Times*, May 11, 1994, p. A16.

[78]   "Numerous instances of the application of senatorial courtesy are on record, with the practice at least partially accounting for rejection of several nominations to the Supreme Court." Abraham, *Justices, Presidents and Senators*, pp. 19-20. Senatorial courtesy, Abraham writes, appeared to have been the sole factor in President Grover Cleveland's unsuccessful nominations of William B. Hornblower (1893) and Wheeler H. Peckham (1894), both of New York. Each was rejected by the Senate after Senator David B. Hill (D-NY) invoked senatorial courtesy.

[79]   The President explained that "we did not inform or clear with either the Minnesota or Virginia Senator. They knew nothing about it and we will not do that with any others." U.S. President (Nixon.), "Remarks Announcing the Nomination of Judge Warren Earl Burger To Be Chief Justice of the United States. May 21, 1969," *Public Papers of the Presidents of the United States*, 1969 vol. (Washington, GPO, 1971), p. 391. The President's decision not to inform the home-state Senators of his choice of Burger may have, to some degree, been influenced by the Senators' party affiliation: All four Senators in this case were Democrats. If any of the home-state Senators had been Republicans, President Nixon might well have, at the very least, advised them of his choice beforehand — rather than risk the embarrassment to them which might come if they were shown to be totally excluded from the selection process.

[80]   Ibid., p. 393.

[81]   See, for example, John Ferling, "The Senate and Federal Judges: The Intent of the Founding Fathers," *Capitol Studies,* vol. 2, Winter 1974, p. 66: "Since the convention acted at a time when nearly every state constitution, and the Articles of Confederation, permitted a legislative voice in the selection of judges, it is inconceivable that the delegates could have intended something less than full Senate participation in the appointment process."

[82]    See, for example, Harris, *Advice and Consent*, p. 34: "The debates in the Convention do not support the thesis since advanced that the framers of the Constitution intended that the President should secure the advice — that is, the recommendations — of the Senate or of individual members, before making a nomination."

[83]    Michael J. Gerhardt, *The Federal Appointments Process* (Durham, NC: Duke University Press, 2000), p. 33. The Constitution, Gerhardt adds, "does not mandate any formal prenomination role for the Senate to consult with the president; nor does it impose any obligation on the president to consult with the Senate prior to nominating people to confirmable posts. The Constitution does, however, make it clear that the president or his nominees may have to pay a price if he ignores the Senate's advice." Ibid.

[84]    "Sen. Specter Holds News Conference on Chairmanship of Judiciary Committee," Feb. 24, 2005, CQ Transcript Service, at *[http://www.cq.com]*.

[85]    The term "elevation" in the judicial appointment process also is used to describe the appointment of a lower federal court appointment to a higher judicial position, such as when a U.S. district judge is nominated to be a U.S. court of appeals judge, or when a court of appeals judge is nominated to be a Justice on the Supreme Court.

[86]    As discussed earlier, the five nominations of sitting Associate Justices to be Chief Justice were: (1) President George Washington's nomination of Justice William Cushing in 1796, (2) President William Howard Taft's nomination of Justice Edward D. White in 1910, (3) President Franklin D. Roosevelt's nomination of Justice Harlan Fiske Stone in 1941, (4) President Lyndon B. Johnson's nomination of Justice Abe Fortas in 1968, and (5) President Ronald Reagan's nomination of Justice William H. Rehnquist in 1986. White, Stone and Rehnquist were confirmed by the Senate and assumed the office of Chief Justice. While Cushing was confirmed as well, he declined the appointment. Fortas failed to receive Senate confirmation. See Table 1 at end of this report.

[87]    A news analysis has suggested that, in the event the current Chief Justice, William H. Rehnquist, retires this year, promoting an associate justice would give President George W. Bush "a chance to appoint an ideologically aligned chief justice in addition to bringing in an associate justice." Jeanne Cummings, "Split Decision: Bush Faces Judicial Test," *Wall Street Journal*, Jan. 4, 2005, p. A4. (Hereafter cited as Cummings, "Split Decision".)

[88] For its part, however, the Senate is not precluded from confirming the Associate Justice nomination prior to confirming the Chief Justice nomination. In such an event, the confirmed Associate Justice nominee cannot not assume office until after the Chief Justice nominee has vacated the Associate Justice office — presumably doing so only after having received Senate confirmation. There has been one instance in which such a scenario occurred, involving the June 12, 1941 nominations of Associate Justice Harlan F. Stone to be Chief Justice and of Senator James F. Byrnes of South Carolina to be Associate Justice. The Byrnes nomination was confirmed by the Senate the same day it was received, on June 12, without being referred to committee, *before* the Stone nomination was confirmed, on June 27, 1941. However, Justice Byrnes took the judicial oath of office, on July 8, 1941, only *after* Chief Justice Stone took his judicial oath, on July 3, 1941.

[89] These were the Chief Justice nominations of John Rutledge in 1795 and Charles Evans Hughes in 1930. Both had served as Associate Justices prior to, but not at, the time of their nominations to be Chief Justice — Rutledge from 1790-1791 and Hughes from 1910 to 1916. See Table 1 at the end of this report

[90] Such a consideration concerned President Harry S Truman following the death of Chief Justice Harlan F. Stone on Apr. 22, 1946. At the time, the Court was experiencing an internal feud between Associate Justices Hugo L. Black and Robert H. Jackson, "with the latter publicly accusing the former of blocking his ascendance to the top spot on the Court ...." Abraham, *Justices, Presidents, and Senators,* p. 183. President Truman "quickly perceived that, for the sake of intra-Court comity, he simply could not promote any of the Court's sitting members...." At the advice of retired Chief Justice Charles Evans Hughes and retired Associate Justice Owen Roberts, the President nominated the Secretary of the Treasury, Fred M. Vinson, to be Chief Justice. Vinson "seemed ideal for the position, given his demonstrated administrative and legislative leadership — he was one of the very few members of the bench to have served in all three branches of the federal government." Ibid.

[91] U.S. President (Nixon.), "Remarks Announcing the Nomination of Judge Warren Earl Burger To Be Chief Justice of the United States. May 21, 1969," *Public Papers of the Presidents of the United States,* 1969 vol. (Washington, GPO, 1971), p.394.

[92] Cummings, *Split Decision,* p. A4.

[93]  Henry B. Hogue, "The Law: Recess Appointments to Article III Courts," *Political Science Quarterly,* vol. 34, September 2004, p. 661.

[94]  Specifically, Article II, Section 2, Clause 3 of the U.S. Constitution empowers the President "to fill up all Vacancies that may happen during the Recess of the Senate, by granting Commissions which shall expire at the End of their next Session."

[95]  See "Recess Appointments to the Supreme Court — Constitutional But Unwise?" *Stanford Law Review,* vol. 10, December 1957, pp. 124-146, especially, p. 125, for table of first 11 recess appointments to the Court, including appointment dates and later Senate confirmation dates. The article was published prior to the twelfth recess appointment, President Eisenhower's recess appointment of Potter Stewart as Associate Justice on Oct. 7, 1958. Stewart subsequently received Senate confirmation to that position.

[96]  A special session of the Congress had adjourned on June 26, 1795, and the 1st session of the 4th Congress would not convene until Dec. 7, 1795. U.S. Congress. Joint Committee on Printing, *2003-2004 Official Congressional Directory 108th Congress* (Washington: GPO, 2003), p. 512 (listing "Sessions of Congress"). (Hereafter cited as *Congressional Directory.*)

[97]  See George S. McCowan, Jr., "Chief Justice John Rutledge and the Jay Treaty," *South Carolina Historical Magazine,* vol. 62, January 1961, pp. 10-23. In first paragraph, the author writes, "The purpose of this article is to trace the chain of events by which the question of the appointment of John Rutledge as Chief Justice became inextricably tied to the question of the ratification of the Jay Treaty."

[98]  U.S. Congress, Senate, *Journal of the Executive Proceedings of the Senate,* Washington: Duff Green, 1828), vol. 1, pp. 195-196.

[99]  Maeva Marcus et al., eds., *The Documentary History of the Supreme Court of the United States, 1789-1800,* vol. 1, part 1 ("Appointments and Proceedings") (New York: Columbia University Press, 1985), p. 100.

[100]  Ibid.

[101]  *Congressional Directory,* p. 512.

[102]  James Reston, "U.S. Mourns Vinson; Delicate Balance of Court at Stake," *New York Times,* Sept. 9, 1953, p. 1.

[103]  At first, after the creation of the Judiciary Committee in 1816, the Senate referred nominations to the Committee by motion only. As a result, until after the Civil War, no more than perhaps one out of three

Supreme Court nominations was sent to the Judiciary Committee for initial consideration. In 1868, however, the Senate determined that all nominations should be referred to appropriate standing committees. Subsequently up to the present day, almost all Supreme Court nominations have been referred to the Judiciary Committee. U.S. Congress, Senate Committee on the Judiciary, *History of the Committee on the Judiciary, United States Senate, 1816-1981*. Senate Document No. 97-18, 97th Congress., 1st sess. (Washington: GPO, 1982), p. iv. After 1868, however, an important exception to the practice of referring Supreme Court nominees to the Judiciary Committee usually was made for nominees who, at the time of their nomination, were current or former Members of the U.S. Senate. CRS Report RL31989, *Supreme Court Appointment Process,* pp. 17-18. Another nomination not referred to the Judiciary Committee was President Warren G. Harding's nomination of former President William Howard Taft to be Chief Justice, which was received by the Senate on June 30, 1921, and confirmed the same day. See "Ex-President Taft Succeeds White as Chief Justice," *New York Times,* July 1, 1921, p. 1.

[104] Roy M. Mersky, Tarlton Law Library, University of Texas at Austin Law School, telephone conversation with the author, Apr. 3, 2003. Professor Mersky and J. Myron Jacobstein have jointly compiled 19 volumes of Senate Judiciary Committee hearings transcripts and reports for Supreme Court nominations, starting with the Brandeis nomination in 1916 and carrying through the most recent Court nomination of Stephen G. Breyer in 1994. See Roy M. Mersky and J. Byron Jacobstein, comp., *The Supreme Court of the United States: Hearings and Reports on Successful and Unsuccessful Nominations of Supreme Court Justices by the Senate Judiciary Committee, 1916-1994,* 19 vols. (Buffalo, NY: William S. Hein & Co., 1977-1996). (Hereafter cited as Mersky and Jacobstein, *Supreme Court Nominations: Hearings and Reports.*)

[105] See James A. Thorpe, "The Appearance of Supreme Court Nominees Before the Senate Judiciary Committee," *Journal of Public Law,* vol. 18, 1969, pp. 371-384. (Hereafter cited as Thorpe, "Appearance of Nominees.") See also David Gregg Farrelly, "Operational Aspects of the Senate Judiciary Committee," (Ph.D. diss., Princeton University, 1949), pp. 184-199, in which author examines the procedures followed by the committee in its consideration of 15 Supreme Court nominations referred to it between 1923 and 1947. The author

observes, on p. 192, that six of the 15 nominations were "confirmed without benefit of public hearings. Of the remaining nine nominations, full public hearings were used on two occasions, another appointee received a limited hearing, and six were given routine hearings. Only [John J.] Parker and [Felix] Frankfurter received full, open hearings." A "routine hearing," the author explained, on pp. 194-195, "differs from a full, open hearing in that a date is set for interested parties to appear and present evidence against confirmation. In other words, a meeting is scheduled without requests for one; an open invitation is extended by the committee for the filing of protests against an appointment." In 1930, although Supreme Court nominee John J. Parker had communicated his willingness to testify, the Judiciary Committee voted against inviting him to do so. "Committee, 10 to 6, Rejects Parker," *The New York Times,* April 22, 1930, pp. 1, 23.

[106]  See transcripts of Feb. 2 and 19, 1954 hearings on nomination of Earl Warren to be Chief Justice, in Mersky and Jacobstein, *Supreme Court Nominations: Hearings and Reports*, vol. 5.

[107]  See "Senators Consider Warren Nomination," *New York Times*, Feb. 3, 1954, p. 16; "Deadline Set for Warren Critics to File," *Washington Post*, Feb. 16, 1954; and "Unsworn Charges Against Warren Stir Senate Clash," *New York Times,* Feb. 20, 1954, p. 1.

[108]  Thorpe, "Appearance of Nominees," pp. 384-402.

[109]  *Congressional Quarterly Almanac 90th Congress 2$^{nd}$ Session . . . 1968*, vol. 24 (Washington: Congressional Quarterly Service, 1968), p. 532.

[110]  Supreme Court confirmation hearings were opened to gavel-to-gavel television coverage for the first time in 1981, when the committee instituted the practice at the confirmation hearings for nominee Sandra Day O'Connor. CRS Report RL31989, *Supreme Court Appointment Process*, p. 19.

[111]  CRS Report RL31989, *Supreme Court Appointment Process*, p. 26. This committee tradition was reaffirmed by the committee's chairman, Sen. Patrick J. Leahy (D-VT), and its ranking minority member, Sen. Orrin G. Hatch (R-UT), in a June 29, 2001 letter to Senate colleagues. The committee's "traditional practice," the letter said, was to report Supreme Court nominees to the Senate, even in cases where the nominees were opposed by a majority of the Judiciary Committee. "We both recognize and have every intention," their letter continued, "of following the practices and precedents of

the committee and the Senate when considering Supreme Court nominees." Sen. Patrick J. Leahy and Sen. Orrin G. Hatch, "Dear Colleague" letter, June 29, 2001, *Congressional Record*, daily ed., vol. 147, June 29, 2001, p. S7282.

[112] CRS Report RL31989, *Supreme Court Appointment Process*, p. 27.

[113] See CRS Report RL32013, *The History of the Blue Slip in the Senate Committee on the Judiciary, 1917-Present*, by Mitchel A. Sollenberger.

[114] U.S. Congress, Senate Committee on the Judiciary, *Nomination of William H. Rehnquist To Be Chief Justice of the United States,* 99th Cong., 2nd sess., Exec. Rept. 99-18 (Washington: GPO, 1986), p.1.

[115] "The Supreme Court of the United States," debate in the Senate, *Congressional Record,* vol. 115, June 9, 1969, pp. 15174-75 and 15192-94. Shortly after this discussion, the Senate concluded debate and voted to confirm the Burger nomination, 74-3. Subsequent to the Burger nomination in 1969, the Judiciary Committee has reported a Supreme Court nomination to the Senate only once without a written report, doing so in December 1975, when it reported favor the nomination of John Paul Stevens to the Court. The absence of a written committee report was not mentioned during very brief Senate consideration of the Sevens nomination, which ended in a 98-0 confirmation vote.

[116] As with other nominations listed in the Executive Calendar, information about a Supreme court nomination will include the name and office of the nominee, the name of the previous holder of the office, and whether the committee reported the nomination favorably, unfavorably, or without recommendation. Business on the Executive Calendar, which consists of treaties and nominations, is considered in executive session. Unless voted otherwise by the Senate, executive sessions are open to the public.

[117] See CRS General Distribution Memorandum, *Criteria Used by Senators To Evaluate Judicial Nominations*, by Denis Steven Rutkus, June 14, 2002, 23 p. (available from author).

[118] Sen. Joseph R. Biden, Jr., "Nomination of William H. Rehnquist To Be Chief Justice of the Untied States," debate in the Senate, *Congressional Record,* daily ed., vol. 132, Sept. 11, 1986, p. S12381.

[119] Ibid.

[120] Sen. Orrin G. Hatch, "Nomination of William H. Rehnquist To Be Chief Justice of the Untied States," debate in the Senate, *Congressional Record,* daily ed., vol. 132, Sept. 11, 1986, p. S12384.

[121] See *Congressional Record,* vol. 132, Sept. 17, 1986, pp. 23729-23803 (debate and vote to confirm Rehnquist) and pp. 23803-23813 (debate and vote to confirm Scalia).

[122] "It was clear that the committee would take no action on Thornberry until the Fortas nomination was settled." Robert Shogan, *A Question of Judgment: The Fortas Case and the Struggle for the Supreme Court* (Indianapolis: The Bobbs-Merrill Company, 1972), p. 172.

[123] Byrnes benefitted from "the unwritten rule of the all but automatic approval of senatorial colleagues." Abraham, *Justices, Presidents, and Senators,* p. 33.

[124] Immediately prior to the Senate's roll-call vote in 1994 on whether to confirm Stephen G. Breyer to be an Associate Justice, Majority Leader George J. Mitchell (D-ME), stated to his colleagues on the floor that "it has been the practice that votes on Supreme Court nominations are made from the Senator's desk. I ask that Senators cast their votes from their desks during this vote." *Congressional Record*, vol. 140, July 29, 1994, p. 18704.

[125] The most recent voice votes on Supreme Court nominations were those by the Senate confirming the Associate Justice nominations of Abe Fortas in 1965 and Arthur J. Goldberg and Byron R. White, both in 1962.

[126] See Table 1 at end of this report.

[127] See, in Table 1 at end of this report, the Chief Justice nominations of George H. Williams in 1873, Caleb Cushing in 1874 and Abe Fortas in 1968. For more complete details on the procedural actions taken on each prior to their withdrawal by the President (including committee hearings dates, committee votes and recommendations, and dates of Senate debate), see CRS Report RL31171, *Supreme Court Nominations Not Confirmed, 1789-2004,* by Henry B. Hogue, pp. 18-23. For short narrative histories on these unsuccessful nominations, see J. Myron Jacobstein and Roy M. Mersky, *The Rejected: Sketches of the 26 Men Nominated for the Supreme Court but Not Confirmed by the Senate* (Milpitas, CA: Toucan Valley Publications, 1993), pp. 82-87 (Williams), 87-93 (Cushing) and 125-137 (Fortas).

[128] Since the 1960s, the closest roll calls on whether to confirm a Supreme Court nomination were the 52-48 vote in 1991 confirming Clarence Thomas; the 45-51 vote in 1970 rejecting G. Harrold Carswell; the 45-55 vote in 1969 rejecting Clement Haynsworth Jr.; the 42-58 vote in 1987 rejecting Robert H. Bork; and the 65-33 vote confirming William H. Rehnquist to be Chief Justice in 1986. The

closest roll call vote ever cast on whether to confirm a Supreme Court nomination was the 24-23 vote in 1881 confirming President James A. Garfield's nomination of Stanley Matthews. Two other Senate votes on Supreme Court nominations decided by one vote were procedural votes which effectively defeated the nominations in question — specifically, a 26-25 vote in 1853 on a motion to postpone consideration of President Millard Fillmore's nomination of George E. Badger and the 25-26 vote in 1861 on a motion to proceed to consider President James Buchanan's nomination of Jeremiah S. Black.

[129] Since the 1960s, the most lopsided of these votes have been the unanimous roll calls confirming Harry A. Blackmun in 1970 (94-0), John Paul Stevens in 1975 (98-0), Sandra Day O'Connor in 1981 (99-0), Antonin Scalia in 1986 (98-0), and Anthony M. Kennedy in 1988 (98-0), and the near-unanimous votes confirming Warren E. Burger to be Chief Justice in 1969 (74-3), Lewis F. Powell Jr., in 1971 (89-1), and Ruth Bader Ginsburg in 1993 (96-3).

[130] U.S. Congress, Senate, *Journal of the Executive Proceedings of the Senate* (Washington: GPO, 1887), vol. 4, p. 520 (proceedings of Mar. 14 and 15, 1836).

[131] See discussion of Fortas episode in next section of this report, under "Filibusters and Motions To Close Debate."

[132] For a more complete discussion of the use of extended debate in the Senate as a tactic to delay or prevent floor votes on nominations, see CRS Report RL32878, *Cloture Attempts on Nominations*, by Richard S. Beth. (Hereafter cited as CRS Report RL32878, *Cloture Attempts.)*

[133] It has only been since 1949, under Senate rules, that cloture could be moved on nominations. Prior to 1949, dating back to the Senate's first adoption of a cloture rule in 1917, cloture motions could be filed only on legislature measures. CRS Report RL32878, *Cloture Attempts*, p. 2.

[134] Prior to 1975, the majority required for cloture was two-thirds of Senators present and voting. Ibid., *Cloture Attempts*, p. 4.

[135] "Supreme Court of the United States," *Congressional Record*, vol. 114, Oct. 1, 1968, pp. 28926-28933. The 45 votes in favor of cloture fell far short of the super-majority required — then two-thirds of Senators present and voting.

[136] Following his withdrawal of the Fortas nomination, as well as the nomination of Homer Thornberry to succeed Fortas as Associate Justice, President Johnson stated that he "deeply regretted" that "the

Senate filibuster prevented the Senate from voting on the nomination of Justice Fortas. Had the Senate been permitted to vote, I am confident that both Justice Fortas and Judge Thornberry would have been confirmed. Their qualifications are indisputable." U.S. President. (Johnson, L.), "Statement by the President Upon Declining To Submit an Additional Nomination for the Office of Chief Justice of the United States. October 10,1968," *Public Papers of the Presidents of the United States — Lyndon B. Johnson,* 1968-69 volume, book 1 (Washington: GPO, 1970), p. 1024.

[137] *Congressional Quarterly Almanac 90th Congress 2nd Session . . . 1968,* vol. 24 (Washington: Congressional Quarterly Service, 1968), p. 536. See also Ronald J. Ostrow, "Dirksen Shifts on Fortas Filibuster," *Los Angeles Times,* Sept. 28, 1968, pp. 1, 5 (noting, on p. 1, that the cloture motion filed by 23 Senators sought "to end prolonged debate on a motion merely to consider the nomination."

[138] "Cloture Motion," *Congressional Record,* vol. 117, Dec. 10, 1971, pp. 46110-46117.

[139] "Nomination of William H. Rehnquist To Be Chief Justice of the United States," *Congressional Record,* vol. 132, Sept. 17, 1986, pp. 23729-23739.

[140] Senate Republican leaders announced that their move to amend Senate rules to bar filibusters against judicial nominations would occur in conjunction with their efforts to close floor debate on the nomination of Priscilla Owen to be a U.S. circuit court of appeals judge. (An earlier nomination of Owen to the same judgeship, during the 108th Congress, had been filibustered successfully by Senate Democrats four times.) Keith Perine and Daphne Retter, "Judicial Showdown Starts with Owen," *CQ Today,* vol. 41, May 18, 2005.

[141] Charles Babington and Shailagh Murray, "A Last-Minute Deal on Judicial Nominations," *The Washington Post,* May 24, 2005, pp. A1, A4.

[142] Several Senate Democrats, it was reported in 2002, had said "they would consider staging a filibuster if President Bush nominates to the high court a conservative not to their liking." Matthew Tully, "Senators Won't Rule Out Filibuster of High Court Nominees," *CQ Daily Monitor,* March 21, 2002, p. 7. More recently, in June 2003, another Democratic Senator declared that he would filibuster any Supreme Court nominee that he found objectionable based on certain specified criteria. Adam Nagourney, "Senator Ready To Filibuster

over Views of Court Pick," *The New York Times,* June 21, 2003, p. A13.

[143] For analysis of the possible courses of action in which Senate rules might be changed to curtail the use of filibusters against judicial nominations, see CRS Report RL32684, *Changing Senate Rules: The 'Constitutional' or 'Nuclear' Option,* by Betsy Palmer. For analysis of whether Senate filibusters of judicial nominations are constitutional, see CRS Report RL32102, *Constitutionality of a Senate Filibuster of a Judicial Nomination,* by Jay R. Shampansky.

[144] This career, after graduation from Harvard Law School in 1979, included the following professional experience: clerk to a U.S. Court of Appeals judge (1979-1980); clerk to then-Associate Justice William H. Rehnquist (1980-1981); special assistant to Attorney General William French Smith (1981-1982); Associate White House Counsel (1982-1986); associate at the Washington, D.C. law firm of Hogan & Hartson (1986-1989); Principal Deputy Solicitor General (1989-1993); partner at Hogan& Hartson (1993-2003); and judge on the U.S. Court of Appeals for the District of Columbia Circuit (2003-present).

[145] See "President Nominates Judge Roberts to be Supreme Court Chief Justice," Sept. 5, 2005 White House News release, including text of the nomination announcement, available at *[http://www.white house.gov/news/releases/2005/09/print/20050905.html].*

[146] Justice O'Connor on July 1, 2005, had announced that she would retire effective upon the confirmation of her successor. On July 19, 2005, President Bush announced his selection of John Roberts to succeed Justice O'Connor, formally nominating Judge Roberts 10 days later, on July 29, 2005.

[147] During this phase, the nominee had completed and returned a detailed judicial nominee questionnaire to the Senate Judiciary Committee, the American Bar Association's Standing Committee on Federal Judiciary completed its investigation of Judge Roberts and transmitted its rating of the nominee to the Senate Judiciary Committee, the nominee had paid "courtesy call" visits on Capitol Hill to many of the Senate's Members, and the Judiciary Committee's members and staff had studied thousands of pages of background information compiled about the nominee, including memoranda and other papers, newly released by the National Archives, which were written by the nominee while a Department of Justice attorney or

White House attorney during the presidential administrations of
Ronald Reagan and George H.W. Bush.

[148]   Peter Baker, "Second Court Vacancy Triggers a Scramble; Bush
Considers Picking Roberts as Chief, Officials Say," *Washington Post*,
Sept. 5, 2005, p. A1.

[149]   See footnote 145.

[150]   See Christopher Lee, "Hill Veterans Light the Way for Nominee,"
*Washington Post*, Sept. 9, 2005, p. A23, reporting that Democratic
members on the Senate Judiciary Committee "say they will press him
[Roberts] harder at his confirmation hearings beginning Monday, now
that he is in line to Chief;" Alexander Bolton, "Roberts Hearing
Delayed," *The Hill,* Sept. 6, 2005, p. 1, reporting that each
Democratic member on the Judiciary Committee will "grill" Judge
Roberts on a specific area of the law or his record. See also CRS
Report RL32821, *Proper Scope of Questioning of Supreme Court
Nominees: The Current Debate,* by Denis Steven Rutkus.

# INDEX